Jonas Mekas
Shiver of Memory

Peter Delpeut

Jonas Mekas Shiver of Memory

Peter Delpeut

Originally published by
Uitgeverij Atlas Contact, Amsterdam

Book design:
Tauras Stalnionis

Publisher's Cataloging-in-Publication Data

Names: Delpeut, Peter, author.
Title: Jonas Mekas , shiver of memory / by Peter Delpeut.
Description: Includes bibliographical references.
| Los Angeles, CA: DoppelHouse Press, 2022.
Identifiers: LCCN: 2021952736 | ISBN: 978-1-954600-03-4
(paperback) | 978-1-954600-04-1 (ebook)
Subjects: LCSH Mekas, Jonas, 1922-2019. | Motion pictures-
-Production and direction--Biography. | Lithuanian
American artists--United States. | Holocaust, Jewish
(1939-1945)--Lithuania. | BISAC BIOGRAPHY & AUTOBIOGRAPHY
/ Artists, Architects, Photographers | ART / Individual
Artists / Essays | ART / Film & Video | HISTORY / Holocaust
Classification: LCC PN1998.3.M44 D45
2022 | DDC 791.43/015--dc23

DoppelHouse Press
Los Angeles
DoppelHouse.com

for Sarah & Chris

Veltui
einu
einu
ir
šen,
ir
ten –

vis
atgal
sugrįžtu,
ir
viskas,
kas
viduj
plyšta
ir
išeiti
veržias,
veržias,

palieka
neat-
verta,
neišsakyta.

Aimlessly
pacing,
going
this
way
and
that,

just
to keep
coming
back,
while
everything
inside,
breaking
and
raging
raging
to escape,

stays
locked up,
un
-told.

from: "Miške / In the Woods," Jonas Mekas, *Words Apart and others: poems 1967 & 1998*
translated from Lithuanian by Vyt Bakaitis.

memories

First a memory (in a memory). It was raining and the streets of Vicenza were deserted. The Sunday flaneurs were hiding in the coffee houses and we fled into the Palazzo Chiericati, one of Palladio's architectural masterpieces that are the pride of the city. The interior turned out to be disappointingly smoothed with white museum walls, but centuries of Italian painting quickly made us forget about it. We were the only visitors and perhaps it was the ascetic silence that held me for a long time in a narrow room, almost a corridor, where a row of "Madonna and Child" were presented, like the ones that were delivered on the assembly line in Italy around 1500. Mary holding the Savior as a still fragile, (half) naked baby on her lap.

I kept coming back to the small paintings by Bartolomeo Montagna, who I didn't know, but of whom I now know that he worked in Giovanni Bellini's studio. The latter perhaps explains the introverted softness in the eyes of the Madonnas, although it was not their gaze that bound me to them. It is only natural to describe the way Mary holds her baby as affectionate, but I saw something else in it: anxiety. For me, her grip was that of a worried mother who wants to protect her child from the dangers that lie ahead. I felt the hand of my own mother, sickly worried: Not too close to the stairwell! Careful crossing! Beware! Attention! She pulled her children tight against her, we threatened to disappear into her skirts, her hand pressed on our chests: loving, no doubt, but also filled with an uncontrollable fear.

There was an explanation for this pathological anxiety, a family story that was often repeated. Her sister, seven years old, had run off the yard of her parents' home carefree and was killed by a cyclist. The memory of this had nested in my mother, just as a body remembers a rotten mussel. Every unexpected movement of her children evoked the image of her running sister — and her lifeless body on the chilly paving stones. She could still tell it sixty, seventy years later with her voice squeezed shut. It was an indestructible emotion, which after all these years still sounded raw. It was her way to clarify the anxiety her children despised: who else but she knew what could happen to us if she didn't protect us?

Why did these Madonnas bring that memory to me right now? My mother passed away many years ago, and I would like to believe that I have left the anguished care for her children behind me. It was not so much the image of my mother that forced itself on me, but a photo from our family album. Together we are waiting along the side of the street for a parade to pass our house. She holds me pressed against her, half bent over because I am still a toddler, and she has put her hand on my chest. The hands of Mary of Montagna and the hand of my mother in the little black and white picture were glued tightly together. Two images – centuries apart – blended into one memory. I was surprised that it could interfere so easily in a carefree museum visit.

My beloved came to see where I was. No more than a glance of understanding, because she knows my penchant for loitering. Look at the hands, I said. When we get home I have to show you a picture.

Back in the Netherlands I wrote an email to my younger sister who keeps the family albums. I described the photo to her and asked her to send it to me. Oh, of course, she mailed me back, I know that picture very well. Only it's not you in it, it's me. The digital image she sent me made any argument superfluous.

It's a well-known fact that we can make other people's memories our own. Not that we always realize that. I was shocked when the picture appeared on my screen, stunned by my wrongful appropriation. My sister didn't feel robbed at all. She pointed out to me that I had spoken about this photo at my mother's funeral, so it had to mean a lot to us. When she wrote that, I remembered that at the end of that ceremony many visitors had come to me to confirm that I had identified something in that photo that summed up my mother's character sharply. Through my observation it had become an iconic image, not so much different from how painters thought they should depict Mary's motherly love. Iconic images are of everyone, which is their strength. I had made it into a picture for everybody.

At the same time, in the spirit of that moment, in front of family and friends, the photograph had crept into my emotional household as a memory that was exclusively mine: this was *my* mother, as she had been to *me*. No matter how factually and traceably that photo was pointing to my sister, it had become me in that photo. It was a trace of my existence, anchored as my memory — but not mine.

With my sister's photograph, I had "augmented" my own memories. It helped me understand my relationship with my mother. It's a helpful memory. I won't forget it, because in its compactness — exemplary yet private — it is a clear scene in the story I want to remember of my mother and me.

Not all memories have that characteristic. There are also memories that we forget, until someone points them out to us — and an uncomfortable situation arises: why did the other person remember something I forgot? Not a bit of forgetting, but in a way that makes it seem as if it didn't happen.

Immediately after the film premiere of a filmmaker friend, a woman enthusiastically addressed me. We apparently had collaborated on organizing an exhibition with works of Sergei Parajanov in the Filmmuseum in Amsterdam — I summarize it now, because for the woman the memory was so clear that she immediately recounted details with me without explaining the context. She expected the same clarity from me, but my image remained empty, even during the rest of the reception. Although I regularly searched for the woman's face, my memory refused to cooperate. I felt guilty that I had not been able to answer her enthusiasm. If I had earned a place in the story of her memory, why then had my memory rejected it so rudely?

Now that I write this down, it seems strange to me, because the completely white spot is no longer as empty as it was when I met her. With a slight discomfort I tried to fill the empty sheet during the return journey on the train with at least a few quick-sketched contours. It wasn't difficult to demarcate place and time (I only worked for the Filmmuseum for seven years, although that was more than twenty years ago), and especially by remembering the narrow exhibition space of that time (just like the corridor with Madonna's in Vicenza) I suddenly saw little pictures in front of me, a long row against a white wall, and I vaguely remembered the appearance of two exotic guests (Armenian? Georgian? a man and a woman?)

who were accompanied by an interpreter: she had to be the woman who had spoken to me, but in my memory she was still without a face, even though there was the face of the reception.

Deduction has evoked images, but they are indeterminate, and moreover they are colored, because through the word Armenia and Parajanov's films I see someone in front of me with deer eyes, almond-shaped as they appear in the women in his films and in the portraits painted by the Armenian painter Niko Pirosmani, which I once wrote about. Is that why they appear so easily in my mind's eye? I filled in the color plate of my memory myself, as I do now, because as I write this down, a table in the museum restaurant returns (where we dined with all our guests of course, how special is that?), and even sharper and more intriguing a little book about Parajanov in Cyrillic script, in which pale, red colored photos as in many Soviet publications of those years, a gift — I've walked to my bookcase now and actually, I find the book, although it's not a book: it's a plastic folder with eighteen framed slides of paintings/collages by the filmmaker, turned into magenta, the hue of the passage of time in color photography. A gift that still moves me and which I now look at with some shame: how could I have forgotten this unique little folder?

I can only think of one answer to it. There is a story about Parajanov that is much more familiar. In my memory it has claimed exactly the space I want to make free for him. Once I interviewed him in his room in the Hilton Hotel in Rotterdam, together with my good friend Mart Dominicus. He had left the Soviet Union for the first time, thanks to Gorbachev's glasnost, and was quite confused by all the impressions and the hero-reception at the film festival. An entourage that walked in and out surrounded him. On the bedside tables were cups with melted ice and a lot of whipped cream, which he ate with mice bites. The room service was regularly called for new refreshments and I imagined — very Dutch — the bill the festival would have to pay at the end of his visit.

Parajanov, small in stature but broad-shouldered, was the natural center, the center of attention. A wild, grey beard and above it furious eyes, constantly twinkling, which may have been from the merry flowing alcohol: Bacchus in the Paradise of Abundance. Behind his eyes, or rather in his whole body, was a sense of hysteria. You could tell from everything that the excitement had overwhelmed him. Mart and I had never experienced anything like it. We admired his films and were happy with every word he said, if only we could stay in that hotel room for a while, where fresh whipped cream was still being brought in. I suspect that we were present at a culture shock of a sensitive mind (in his own country a bohemian), of whom it seemed increasingly astounding to us that he could have made his dark, symbol overloaded films within the repressive system of Soviet culture.

We were on one of the highest floors of the hotel, and at the huge windows, wide as a projection screen (which Parajanov kept pointing out to us incessantly), loudly screeching seagulls flew by in the cold January air. They reminded Parajanov of a Belgian film, he said, *Seagulls Die in the Harbor*. A film I had once seen, but I didn't get any further than a black and white image of a harbor quay. Parajanov seemed to remember it all: a sailor dressed in black turtleneck on a deserted quay, and the aimlessness of the hero, who can't decide whether or not to sign up as a sailor, fleeing from the killing of his wife.

Stay or leave, that was the theme of the film. Was Parajanov considering staying in Rotterdam? Was that the hidden message behind that memory?

And now that I'm writing this (writing is a memory machine that seldom fails), all of a sudden the deer eyes appear. Not from one of the guests at the Filmmuseum, but from the Dutch (?) translator in Rotterdam, who certainly wasn't Armenian, but a woman everyone fell in love with that festival year. Which escaped her, I believe, as she was fully immersed in the hours-long sessions with Parajanov and his admirers.

I have never forgotten this Parajanov, and I will probably never forget the interview. I suspect it is an experience that I continue to make more beautiful, more intense than I experienced it in the moment itself. It has become a story, part of the novel my memory over the years of my life has written — and I eagerly tell over and over again. Why am I so sure of this memory? Suppose I checked my memory, could a photograph come up that destroys my image of it?

Such an experiment doesn't have to be very complicated. The interview with Parajanov can be found in *Skrien*, which, because no library has indexed the magazine yet, becomes old-fashioned browsing pages — the dust that swirls up from the old volumes will give my historical research a romantic touch. I can also test my memory against that of Mart, with whom I am still friends, find out what he remembers, what place the event got in the novel of his life. Pieter van der Meer, the court photographer of the Rotterdam Film Festival, gave me a beautiful picture of Parajanov a few months ago, taken in the same year as the interview. The little stocky man with the fiery eyes now looks at me every time I enter the living room. My description of him is based on that photo and not on my memory; I have no illusions about that.

The (almost) forgotten memory of the exhibition in the Filmmuseum can also be checked, although it would require some more work. I could fall back on documents: leaflets, newspaper clippings and, who knows, in the company archives even a memo made by my hand, the names of the guests (and the interpreter!) and also a clarification about the pictures in my memory, which might be collages like the slides in my little folder?

But why would I do that? I'm not waiting for contradiction. The memory of Parajanov in Rotterdam has nestled itself in my memory as a pleasant truth. The exhibition in Amsterdam with the guests from Russia (Moscow, now even forces itself on me, two Armenians from Moscow...) didn't make it to the continuous text of my life. Why should I feel guilty about that? You can't remember every event, and it certainly shouldn't replace the hotel room in the Hilton. It's like a lack of space in my archive — I don't do it very often, but sometimes the paper bin is my last way out.

It all sounds innocent, not something to worry about. But there is one question that worries me and that I never thought about in the time of both events: should I have worried about Parajanov's well-being, or that of my guests from Moscow?

Suppose that our interview with Parajanov would have aroused the interest of Russian secret services and they would as a final convulsion of the disintegrating system have arrested him? His homosexuality (and his colorful entourage) has been used for years as a stick to beat him with. They would have been able to force him to explain his freedom-loving statements once more, and to throw the heroic reception in the free West at his feet, reason enough to imprison him again. Our text, noted in all innocence, could just as well have destroyed his life.

And who were the mysterious guests from Moscow who managed Parajanov's legacy — what rights could they claim? The Wall had fallen, and in Russia there was a gold rush of wild capitalism. Why would the arts have been safeguarded from that? Who knows, I might have participated in an illegal sale of Parajanov's legacy. Shouldn't I have been alert to that?

I speculate freely. We lived in "quiet" times. At least in my memory, for in fact I know nothing about how these two stories fit into the bigger story of Soviet history. I don't feel any urgency to check the archives either, but suppose someone, say a historian, did this? And I would have played a role that I myself was not aware of, and I would have overlooked something that had caused Parajanov or his heirs irreparable suffering? Could my inattention or indifference be blamed on me twenty-five years later?

This happened to the Lithuanian-American filmmaker Jonas Mekas, one of my film heroes since my student years. Only the events neglected by him were hardly imaginable and gruesome in scale, and they took place in a time of war and occupation, putting even more pressure on everything. His past was catching up with him, no matter how much he had tried to keep it out of the novel of his life.

Jonas Mekas

In the summer of 2018, I opened the newest edition of *The New York Review of Books*, as always, curious.

My eye immediately fell on an article about Jonas Mekas. It's not a magazine I read to be informed about film, that's not the strongest point. After just a few paragraphs, I understood that the article wasn't about film, but about the "war past" of the ninety-five-year-old filmmaker. I was shocked. Michael Casper, a young American historian, claimed that in his films, publications and interviews, Mekas had deliberately forgotten or misrepresented important events from his younger years in the Lithuania of the Second World War. Casper had verified Mekas's memories, as he had summarized them in iconic anecdotes. He had come across facts that, in his eyes, contradicted the filmmaker's memory.

Mekas himself, I understood from the article, stuck to his own memories. He didn't make the genuflection that politicians and their spin-doctors usually make in such a matter. No rushing sorry from him. That sounds stubborn. And very much Mekas. With Mekas, his work and his life are inseparable. Subjectivity is central to him, only the now counts and one's own perception of it. That also applies to what we remember from the past. Memories are part of an eternal present. In the eyes of Mekas, Casper could not know anything about his past. He had not been there.

I admired and admire Mekas as a filmmaker. But was that enough to take him at his word? Did I want to go along with his radical idea of subjectivity?

Casper's article sounded convincing. If I accepted his interpretation of Mekas's past, what did that mean for my admiration? Shouldn't my hero deserve my unconditional support? Couldn't the paths of memory have been more unpredictable than Casper suggested? Confusing questions about a figure that had been too important in my formative years to give up just like that.

Jonas Mekas came into my life when, as a timid cinephile, I bought his *Movie Journal* as a remainder for four guilders and fifty cents. It appeared in 1972, and I suspect I bought the discounted paperback (original price 12 guilders and five cents) around 1976. That I bought a book for the price of a cinema ticket from a filmmaker unknown to me must be attributed to my insatiable longing for the unknown and unseen. As a cinephile, I was driven by an appetite for new films, recent or old, but preferably obscure: like any collector, I wanted to be special, to have an exclusive taste for it. That appetite could not really be quenched in Utrecht, the provincial city where I went to the cinema at the time. If I couldn't see everything I wanted to see (even videoshops didn't exist), that could only be compensated with knowledge, which, oh irony, of course only increased the longing for the real images. At the same time, I discovered, reading about film could be as exciting as listening to a radio report of a sporting event. Both appealed to my imagination, and many films (like those matches), which I could observe later, didn't get any poorer.

Movie Journal is a collection of columns Mekas wrote for *The Village Voice*. Starting in the late 1950s, he and the equally legendary Andrew Saris formed the team that was supposed to discuss new cinema releases. Mekas withdrew from that. He preferred to stay in back rooms where incomprehensible films were shown to a handful of enthusiasts. Regular film criticism didn't have his heart. The subtitle of the collection is *The Rise of a New American Cinema, 1959–1971*, but that, too, offers no support. It is anything but a classic film history, for which the pieces react too much to daily current affairs.

His columns were nothing more than a public diary. They were about everything that Mekas had noticed in a week in cinemas, on film sets of friends, or at hip film premieres. His pieces still read like a chronicle of the New York avant-garde, where in his view experimental filmmakers deserved more attention than what the big studios thought they should release. Reading Mekas is like being present, full of the enthusiasm of the moment, and never spoiled by the calm, thoughtful look afterwards.

Reflection is not what drives Mekas, and certainly not the writing of "reviews," "film critiques," in which he mainly resists the word "criticism." "Whoever puts it into our heads that a critic should 'criticize,'" he writes on May 10, 1962, "I have come to a conclusion: The evil and the ugliness will take care of themselves; it is the beautiful and good that need our care." Admiration, unconditional admiration, that's what Mekas likes to put his energy into. Admiration of actually everything that is projected on a film screen is easy for him. "Didn't you know that, when you think about it, I have almost unlimited taste," he rightly points out on June 28, 1962, to readers who don't understand his unorthodox approach. "I can enjoy the poetry of Brakhage, the silent movies of Griffith and Eisenstein, the movies of Hawks and Ulmer, the pornographic flicks of Hoboken, the films of Vanderbeek, the psychiatric films shown at Cinema 16, the Westerns shown only on 42nd Street, and, depending on my mood, practically anything that moves on the screen? I had one of my most exciting evenings of cinema while watching somebody's home movies taken with an 8 mm camera on a trip across the country." With the latter he seems to be pointing ahead to the films he will make himself.

I recognized in Mekas a film buff whom I wanted to emulate. What was new to me was that he dared to link his unlimited taste without restraint to his own unlimited personality. Every review of a film should be individual, he claimed, because everyone experiences a film differently. "Don't you know that anything that moves on the screen can have some meaning for someone in the audience," he rhetorically points out to his readers (and fellow film critics). Every body is different, every one of us has his or her own history, and the projections on cinema screens mingle with that. For Mekas, there is no dividing line between film and life. Both are equally real. They form a cheerful or melancholic tangle (for each of us, it will be a different one), but as Mekas writes about it, this entanglement is self-evident.

I've always looked at *Movie Journal* in my bookcase with a certain melancholy. In every life, there are times when someone needs to put a hand on your shoulder. For the young, still inquisitive cinephile that I was, Mekas fulfilled that role, with a book of ancient columns. When most of my film books disappeared behind doors, and I didn't even bother to sort them out any more, *Movie Journal* remained visible. After all, it contains the lessons I still take to heart. Expressing admiration is many times more difficult than formulating criticism. Every film and every work of art has its own raison d'être, it only needs to mean something to one person. And most important of all: I want art and life to go together. I have always tried to make films, books, paintings, plays and musical performances an integral part of my existence. As a simple pleasure, as a challenge, as a troublemaker, as a consolation, and as a pleasure that stimulates the senses, triggers thinking, it enraptures my body.

That is how I have known him for a long time, that crazy Jonas from New York, who surprised, encouraged and reassured me with his remaindered book: I was on the right track. The book remained an anchor point in my bookcase, which I didn't have to grab, because a glance at the solid chocolate letters on the spine was enough to know what it had started with.

If I had been in New York in the 1970s, when I bought *Movie Journal*, on Broadway at Broome Street, I would have met the lanky figure of Jonas Mekas there. He was on his way to Wooster Street, where he had a studio in one of the loft buildings that his friend and Fluxus leading man George Maciunas had converted into artists' cooperatives. In the Fluxhouse Coop at number 80 he ran his own *cinemathèque* and film archive, a long-standing dream that had finally gained a foothold. In the evening he would visit a theater show of the Wooster Group in The Performing Garage, or on the corner of Wooster and Broome a multimedia jazz concert in The Kitchen.

SoHo was not yet the chic shopping district that it is today, but an artists' village where the lofts had been discovered not only as a studio, but also as residential spaces. Mekas would greet everyone he met, certainly all the artists, from Christo to Nam June Paik, from Donald Judd to Yoko Ono, just like the filmmakers who lived and worked there, the writers and musicians. They too would greet him enthusiastically, the man with the camera who always filmed, when there was a wedding of friends, the opening of a new gallery, or a protest march on Broadway, for whatever good cause. And when he met Jackie Kennedy on the street, she too would greet him with open arms – the charming appearance in her bright red coat had a soft spot for him. If George Maciunas could be called the "Father of SoHo," responsible for the gentrification of the old factory district, then Jonas Mekas was the unelected mayor.

Mekas's *Movie Journal* had the tone of a born New Yorker, so easily he moved in the art scene of those days. It wasn't until later, when I saw his films, that I understood that this had been preceded by an eventful history. Mekas was an exile, which, in hindsight, might also be less surprising: most cultural communities need outsiders to bring about revolutions. Mekas was such an outsider with a special biography.

He was born on December 24, 1922. Not in the United States, but in the "old" Europe. His birthplace was in Semeniškiai, a hamlet not far from the Lithuanian-Russian border, about 15 kilometers from the larger Biržai, where he went to secondary school and when he didn't work on his parents' farm, he sometimes had jobs. The young Mekas was a student and a poet during first the Soviet invasion of 1940 (as a result of Stalin's pact with Hitler) and then the occupation by the Germans (after what is known as Operation Barbarossa). Just before the Soviet troops were to march into Lithuania again, he fled to Germany with his younger brother Adolfas, convinced they would be able to study in Vienna. The flight ended in Hamburg, where both brothers were put to work as forced labor in an airplane factory.

After the German capitulation, he and his brother did not want to return to a Lithuania that was part of the Soviet Union, although their parents and three brothers and a sister were left behind there. They stayed for years as Displaced Persons in German refugee camps in both the British and American zones, until they were able to emigrate to the United States in 1949. There, Mekas became the tireless key figure and hero of New York's avant-garde cinema, editor-in-chief and publisher of the cult magazine *Film Culture*, columnist for *The Village Voice*, and founder of The Film-Makers' Coop and the legendary Anthology Film Archives. He was friends with all the greats of what became known as the New American Cinema and with many celebrities, for whom he had a fine nose (he even counted Jackie Kennedy among his friends). And he made movies. Quirky films, all circling around the theme of remembrance.

Mekas was obsessed with preserving memories from an early age. Before he documented his life on celluloid almost every day in America, he kept a written diary, also during the war years. Parts of this diary, which he wrote from between July 19, 1944, and August 20, 1955, were published in an English translation in 1991 as *I Had Nowhere to Go*. In the introduction, Mekas recalled his youth in Lithuania: the arbitrariness of the deportations under the

Soviet regime, the relative calm during the German occupation, his fear of being betrayed for his modest contribution to underground activities, and his dream of being a poet.

In 1972, he made a film about his first visit to Lithuania after his emigration, *Reminiscences of a Journey to Lithuania*, in which his mother turns out to still live under primitive conditions in the Lithuanian countryside. The lack of running water in the small farm shocks the New York bohemian, although he likes to avoid willingly adapting to the peasant life he once left. Four years later, in *Lost, Lost, Lost*, he told the story of his emigration to the U.S. and the first impressions of the promised land that he had captured with his Bolex camera, which he purchased soon after his arrival. Both films are drenched in nostalgia.

When they were shown at festivals, I liked to walk into them. Not necessarily to watch them until the end, but just to get some antidote for all those propulsive, narrative, inescapable films that don't give you the time or the freedom to mirror your own thoughts or memories. Watching his films is an intimate gathering, as if he has shot his images only for you and projected them on a pale white wall in his own loft exclusively for you.

Mekas continued to write poems in Lithuanian all his life. He wrote his collection *Semeniškių idilės* (translated as *Idylls of Semeniškiai*) in 1947, as a

Displaced Person in Germany. In Lithuania it is considered a classic. Mekas sings of his native land in a stream of lyrical memories: of the landscape, the comings and goings of the seasons, the tools to work the land, the faces of family members, neighbors, passers-by. It is an attempt to hold onto what his memories are in danger of losing their grip on, a nostalgia that still works in the English translation. In any case, the lost paradise of youth never seems far away when Mekas begins to narrate. A paradise abruptly taken away from him by the events of the Great World History, in which Lithuania was a plaything of two totalitarian powers.

I've always perceived it as a beautifully clear life story. As I read and heard more about it over the years, it added urgency to Mekas's status as an experimental filmmaker: exile, nostalgia, displaced, longing for what has been lost, an obsessive cherishing of sweet memories, victim of both communism and Nazism. This was a man who had been through something and nevertheless devoted his life unselfishly to a vulnerable cinema. The writer of *Movie Journal* did not come out of nowhere. His cinematographic playfulness took place on the surface of a rough canvas. I wasn't the only one who thought about it that way. Especially in his last years — he died on January 23, 2019, at ninety-six years old — Mekas was venerated in cinephile circles as a saint, not least in "liberated"

Lithuania, which had finally emerged from the Soviet yoke and embraced their prodigal son.

Like everyone else, I saw no reason to doubt Mekas's story: hadn't he written it all down in his diaries and told it in his films? Until Michael Casper, in the prestigious *The New York Review of Books*, questioned the part of the story that had taken place during the Second World War. Suddenly I had to wonder if Mekas, the man who wanted to share everything with his audience, had withheld things from me. It put a bomb under the intimacy that I thought I could believe in during the screenings of his film.

Michael Casper

Maybe Mekas has been struck by bad luck. If Michael Casper had not come up with the idea of setting up a new historical research project under the title "Life During Wartime: Biržai and the Holocaust in the Lithuanian Heartland" that would examine the period through Mekas's diaries and films, he would have escaped the verification of his memories.

Casper must have seen Mekas initially as the perfect informant for his project. More than seventy years after the World War, he was still lucid and approachable and also known as someone who had meticulously documented his personal life, on paper and on celluloid — a living memory, who resided in

New York. But after extensive archive research in Lithuania and several conversations and exchanges of correspondence, Casper felt he had to contradict Mekas's memories. Moreover, he identified omissions that he did not want to attribute to innocent forgetfulness. Although Mekas stubbornly tried to stick with his memories, or was spurred on by Casper's irrefutable documents to adjust them just as stubbornly, there was no holding on: Mekas's memory, which for seventy years seemed like that of a reliable witness to Lithuania in wartime, lost credibility per stretching meter — at least in Casper's eyes.

The New York Review of Books published Casper's findings in the issue of June 7, 2018, under the title "I Was There." In the sidebar the article is linked to the reissue of *I Had Nowhere to Go* (initiated by Scottish artist Douglas Gordon, who made a film about it) and three recent editions: *A Dance with Fred Astaire*, a new collection of anecdotes, and the first edition of the war diaries of Mekas's brother Adolfas, *The Adolfas Diaries Book 1: September 1941–December 1946* and *The Adolfas Diaries Book 2: February 1947–October 1949*. However, nowhere do you read the intention of a book review. If the article is a review of something, then it is of Mekas himself, of his public role as someone who witnessed the horrors that took place in Lithuania between 1939 and 1945. Is it right, Casper wonders, that Mekas should be honored as an important and selfless witness to this?

Mekas, Casper first of all makes clear, is a witness who doesn't have his facts straight. The chronology of events such as Mekas remembers in diaries, interviews and his films does not match the data he has on hand as a historian. In certain cases this is not difficult to correct and provide years with the right events. Memories tend to clump together, as Casper will have realized. Many of the events from Mekas's stories that cannot be traced in archives or documents turn out to be very difficult to link to dates. In Mekas's mind they have been canonized into the unshakable novel of his life, expressed in a stream of recurring anecdotes. Casper, with his desire for objective, 'historical' dates, finds it difficult to get a grip on them.

He says it nowhere in so many words, but it is clear that Casper wonders whether all this clumping together of Mekas's memories is not a carefully erected smokescreen. You can attribute that to the professional mistrust of the historian, but I can't escape the impression that Casper's sense of detection has gradually been fed by irritation. After all, why does Mekas seem to systematically avoid one event in the anecdotes he so often recites: the fate of his neighbors – the Lithuanian Jews?

The history of the Lithuanian Jews was more or less new to me. If I knew anything about it, it certainly wasn't because of what I could have learned from Mekas's work. Casper summarizes it tersely.

Immediately after the German invasion of Lithuania, on June 22, 1941, the Nazis started to gather Jewish citizens in ghettos, only to start a mass murder not long after. Within a few months, over ninety percent of the Jewish community was murdered and left behind in mass graves. German SS officers were in charge, but were assisted by Lithuanian police and civilians, largely recruited under support of Lietuvos Aktyvistų Frontas (the Lithuanian activist front, or LAF for short), a nationalist movement that welcomed German troops as liberators. Immediately after the invasion, the LAF set up several pro-German regional newspapers, in which, in addition to ordinances from the occupying forces and local news, fierce anti-Semitic articles appeared. These publications, as historians have argued, contributed to the efficiency with which the mass murder could be carried out.

The young Mekas publishes poems in two weekly magazines founded by the LAF. Casper discovers that they can be read alongside calls to cleanse Lithuania from the Jews. Casper hurries to emphasize that he has not found any anti-Semitic statements by Mekas. Regionalist natural lyricism, that's what the poet Mekas writes. Mekas claims (a bit too hastily?) never to have heard of the LAF. They were magazines like the ones that appeared in those days.

Mekas is also otherwise closely involved with the magazines: as (deputy) editor-in-chief of the one in Biržai and in the more technical function of final editor of the one in Panevėžys. When Casper submits to him the disputed anti-Semitic and pro-German articles, he fails to remember them. Moreover, he adjusts earlier statements by saying that he bragged a little about his role with the magazines.

My first thought was that the ambitious adolescent had allowed himself to be seduced by a press that had been brought into line with the occupying forces. It must have been difficult for the farmer's son to resist the possibility of working on a real magazine and publishing poems in it. Perhaps he should have known better, recognizing the poison of the LAF as more than idealistic nationalism. But if he wanted to keep his precious little job, didn't that include making ready for printing the numerous ordinances the Germans published on the front page — those were only alphabet letters of which he hadn't written a single one himself, were they not?

Maybe Casper would have wanted to allow that thought too, if only Mekas had not so ostentatiously kept silent about the one great event that must have visibly and dramatically changed the sight of Biržai in one day. On August 8, 1941, 2,400 Jews were herded together in the center of Biržai and taken in small groups to the Astravas grove in the forest of Pakamponys, not far from the town near the shore of the lake. There they — men, women, children, babies — were shot one by one and dumped in hastily dug pits. In the following days, farmers were ordered to seal the graves and flatten the blood-soaked earth with their carts.

Again for the record: there is no indication that Mekas would have participated in this. Witnesses who knew Mekas as an adolescent could not imagine it either, Casper is told: too dreamy, too much an introvert. But men from his circle of acquaintances did assist in guarding the confiscated possessions of the murdered Jews. Mekas, in turn, says that he saw nothing and that he was not in Biržai during the executioners' day. His memory provides him with three different places of residence. Not that he knows exactly in the end. It's deduction, an attempt to get the chronology in order. His memory leaves him empty-handed, he claims.

One-third of the inhabitants of Biržai disappeared from the face of the earth after that disastrous eighth of August, according to Casper. Their houses, shops and synagogue were left empty. After much research in Mekas's diaries and films, Casper finds only a few, mostly disguised, references to the mass murder in Biržai. It seems, suggests Casper, a hole in his memory that he carefully maneuvers around, a no-go area in his emotional household, black as the lake at which Biržai is situated, black as the tamped earth in the forest of Astravas.

There's more to Casper than irritation. There's also suspicion, if not disbelief. Mekas has always claimed that he left Lithuania in 1944 to study in Vienna. His uncle knew people there who could take care of him. This way he could avoid a call for military service or forced labor. Casper is especially interested in the date of departure, because Mekas only travels when the Soviet army approaches the border of Lithuania. Wasn't that journey prompted rather by the expected invasion? And to study in 1944 in the Third Reich, which was in the process of dissolution, is that really a credible possibility?

Nowhere does Casper formulate these questions explicitly but the suggestion is hard to miss. Mekas's work for the nationalist news magazines would undoubtedly be interpreted by the Soviets as collaboration with the Nazis. In the weeks of the Russian advance, the news magazines placed calls to work for the German war industry in order to contribute to the fight against the Bolsheviks. Mekas must have made those announcements ready for printing. The question that then arises is hardly underlying: has the labor in Hamburg, where Mekas and his brother eventually end up, really been forced? Did he flee with the German retreat?

How eagerly would Casper have wanted to read that through the diaries! Because where are the diaries from before 1944? Destroyed, says Mekas, the openly anti-German and anti-communist sentiments in them could have endangered him. And the originals of *I Had Nowhere to Go*, Casper tries, might he be allowed to see them? Also destroyed, Mekas claims, they had become superfluous after their publication. Could that really be the case, Casper wonders when he takes a look at the filmmaker's apartment. Isn't Mekas the hoarder of his own life, he who carefully collects all the evidence of his conduct? And this Mekas has referred these documents to the wastepaper basket out of everything he could clean up? After an incomplete compilation in English and Lithuanian?

I still summarize it more explicitly than Casper formulated it, which I only realized when I actually put myself to this summary. What smolders suggestively between the lines (and I speak out loud here) occurs to me as carefully directed. Stylistically, it's the cleverness of the article and at the same time its pitfall. Casper treads a slippery path. There are no actual crimes attributable to Mekas. No pro-German or anti-Semitic texts of his can be found. Can Casper blame Mekas for more than a survival strategy that many have pursued: blending in with the occupying forces, cautious resistance, and saving one's own life, if need be by traveling to hated Germany? Why, then, does he find it so important to correct Mekas, and to undermine or question the factuality of his story?

About that, I think Casper leaves no room for misunderstanding. Mekas has kept quiet about what shouldn't be kept quiet about. He writes and talks and films about Lithuania in World War II as if the Holocaust wasn't part of it. There is no place in Mekas's memories for the mass murder of 2,400 Jewish citizens from his immediate surroundings — as a historian of Judaism in Lithuania, Casper cannot forgive him for that.

My own emotions while reading the article were not different. A massacre perpetrated on 2,400 fellow citizens: you can't forget that. A third of the population disappeared in one single day: not to notice such a thing is impossible. To overlook the anti-Semitism of the articles you copy-edit: how ignorant can you pretend to be. Going to study in Vienna while the war is at its height: unlikely.

It was only upon a second reading that I wondered whether to attribute my distrust to my own, sincere indignation or to Casper's stylistic abilities. Casper's approach is that of suggestive dissection, like a public prosecutor who has to rely on purely circumstantial evidence for his trial. First of all, he wants to prove that Mekas did indeed know about the mass murder. To this end, he searches for the snippets that support his disbelief: "... in one 1946 journal entry published in a Lithuanian-language collection, Mekas writes of Lithuanians haunted by the blood-spattered ghosts of Jews they killed and robbed. In *I Had Nowhere to Go*, he mentions that he is afraid to go to a certain pond in the German woods: 'The slightest movement on the dark surface of the pond, the rotten, putrid, black leaves on the bottom. Everything is calling me back, wakening up memories of Astravas and Biržai.' In the final entry, from 1955, he writes of staring across a 'quiet New England lake,' adding, 'I suddenly had a feeling that my past had caught up with my present.... I was sitting there and trembling with memory.'"

Casper reads these snippets as confessions that escaped from a closed compartment of Mekas's memory. And stokes that fire up again. He sends Mekas scans of two pages from the Lithuanian version of his diaries (which do not appear in the English version), in which his compatriots are haunted by ghosts from the past:

> Murderers without iron shackles on their hands and madmen without straitjackets.
>
> Often I think of you. A hundred times I condemn you and a hundred times I acquit you.
>
> And isn't a not-small part of the curse and guilt of what you did also on me?

He asks if Mekas doesn't recognize painful feelings of guilt and complicity in his own writings. Mekas reacts furiously to the suggestion. He's nothing but a poet: "As a poet I feel it deeper even than those who committed those crimes!"

And that's where Casper hits the heart of what he wants to confront Mekas with: "Mekas has been identified so often as a survivor of Nazi persecution that his story has become associated with Jewish 'victimhood.'" In Casper's opinion, Mekas cannot assert any right to this: "... Mekas's experience of the war in Lithuania was nothing like the Jewish one."

Casper points Mekas toward his selective memory. How is it possible that Mekas hardly remembers anything of what in Casper's eyes *should have been* the most traumatic event of his war years: the murder of 2,400 Jews on his doorstep? If you can forget that, what are your other memories worth? With this "big forget-forget trick" Mekas loses the right of victimhood, let alone to exploit it as such. Compared to what has befallen the Jews, it is nothing more than trivialities with which he has acquired his status as a "witness to the horrors of the twentieth century." Mekas, Casper concludes, "has the authority of a witness but none of the responsibility of one." Mekas befits modesty, if not humility, in the face of the Jews murdered in Biržai.

Mekas, in turn, is irritated by Casper's skepticism. Hadn't he been there himself, in Biržai: "... me, who was there? Even if I wasn't fully there?"

Mekas often goes back to that "not fully there." He has, he explains, built a protective wall around events that are too gruesome for him, which doesn't mean that he puts his own memories aside. To him, those memories are still "true," no matter what contradictory facts Casper thinks he can put up against them: "You are talking about 'difficulty to acknowledge the facts,'" Mekas wrote to Casper. "No, it's not for me, not at all. What's difficult is the remembering of the facts themselves. Because there were 'facts'; life consists of 'facts,' but each of us concentrates in our lives only on certain 'facts,' closest to each of us. The rest passes unnoticed, not essential to one's existence, slips out of memory."

With this quote, Casper abruptly ends his article, as if to leave Mekas's defense hanging in the air, above an abyss of which readers are allowed to make their own visualizations. Are there really facts that may go unnoticed to our memory?

It's obvious how Casper feels about that. For him, there are events that simply cannot be allowed to escape memory, even if they are painful and unbearable traumas, even if they didn't happen to you personally. In fact, if you don't dare to look those events in the eye, or don't want to articulate them, then you are depriving yourself of the right to speak about other things. It sounds like the curse that Primo Levi, in his famous poem "Shema," pronounces on those who do not want to pass on the memory of the horrors of the concentration camps to their children (in the translation of Ruth Feldman and Brian Swann):

> Or may your house crumble,
> Disease render you powerless,
> Your offspring avert their faces from you.

The Holocaust and his experiences in Auschwitz made remembrance a duty for Levi. Who dares contradict that? I can well understand that Casper, as a historian of twentieth-century Judaism in Lithuania, identifies with it. After all, the entire project of the Nazis was aimed at erasing that history, as if the Jews in Lithuania (and elsewhere) had never existed — which was more or less achieved in just a few months by murdering over ninety percent of the people who "carried" that history. That is the harrowing side of Casper's role and of all historians dealing with the Holocaust, they are still battling the Nazi legacy with their research.

Yet I found Casper's judgment very harsh. Had Mekas really appropriated the victimhood of the Jews of Lithuania? What kind of victimhood could ever evaporate in the light of the Holocaust? Did that make Mekas's personal odyssey less painful for himself? Can you turn suffering into a contest? No matter how unspeakably huge the suffering inflicted on the Jews, it cannot be used to disqualify someone else's personal suffering. Mekas had been driven from his home and at the very least was a victim of turbulence in history over which he could only have had a minimal influence. It may sound unpleasant, but life takes its turn after even the most horrendous drama, the routine of the day loses itself in trivialities, spelling checks, writing poems, and hoping to publish them. These were the "facts" that had been essential to

Mekas's autobiography.

Moreover, would it not be possible that it was precisely Mekas's silence, if not concealment, that was the real tragedy? When Casper suggests to him in an email that the atrocities couldn't have escaped him, he responds: "I am closed to monstrous events. The Soviet deportations, the holocaust... It's all far beyond the normal human imagination. I react to it abstractly. No emotion. I live in a tightly closed circle drawn around myself." He didn't allow the massacre in the forest of Astravas a place in his memory. Anyone who thinks about memories will always consider at some point the possibility of dissociation.

How pleasant it is that my own memory is very good at forgetting. You can't live permanently with the painful moments of your past. It is hard enough that they sometimes surprise you, or by way of a sixteenth-century painting of "Madonna with child" unexpectedly rise out of the fog. Aren't we all trying to control our memories? And aren't we happiest if we manage to do that? Don't we have the right to forget?

The article urged me to make my own judgment. Casper thought he had enough evidence to know what that verdict would turn out to be. So why did I hesitate?

Friends I presented my dilemma to automatically split into two camps. The fact that Mekas had written for magazines that had been brought into line with the occupying forces was enough for the first group to have — unread — confidence in the historian Casper: Forget? What do you mean? Mekas had been "wrong" in the war and of course he had deliberately concealed the mass murder of the Jews in Biržai. And the "fact" of his concealment easily led to far-reaching suspicion — why wouldn't he have been among the killers?

The second group was less self-assured. They cited the occupation of the Germans as an extenuating circumstance, showed understanding for Mekas's going along with the occupier, and wondered how steadfast they themselves would be in such circumstances. The mass murder, they concluded — likewise unread — was a trauma that Mekas must have repressed. You had to understand that. Condemning Mekas unreservedly was inappropriate.

I noticed that I felt most comfortable with the second group. One of the great lessons of Mekas's *Movie Journal* was that you have to grace every work of art with its existence. Only if you go along with its intentions can you understand and appreciate it. I've always understood that as a life-lesson as well. You have to allow each and every person his or her place. But now I wondered whether that could also apply to their actions, to their acting or not acting in precarious circumstances, when lives are at stake. When does going along become a crime, where lies the demarcation?

It seemed to me a weakness to cover everything

just like that with the cloak of love. At the same time, I wondered what gave me the right at all to judge Mekas (or anyone else), positively or negatively. What could I know of his deepest intentions? What did I know of his "facts"? Didn't his experiences belong to him and nobody else?

And then Casper, what drove him to believe he could morally judge Mekas? What allowed him the arrogance that he believed he could describe the past truthfully? Why could his story claim more general validity than the individual memory of Mekas, who had been there himself?

I reread the article and found no answers. I decided to do my own research. About Mekas, about Casper, and about my own judgments, which were searching diligently for solid ground.

Mekas revisited

It was a strange experience to watch the films of Jonas Mekas again after reading Casper's article. Suddenly, they seemed to pretend to be a fixable rebus, and if I had any sympathy for poor Jonas, all the more so now. It was impossible not to watch all those hours of film as a battle with remembering, as an attempt to outwit memory.

Of course, that has everything to do with the genre in which Mekas worked, about which I never had many thoughts, but that now attracted all the attention. Autobiographical documentaries may be a good first characterization. There is clearly an "I" who films and speaks. The films are always about that "I" and his immediate surroundings, and about "what preceded it," his personal history as a Displaced Person, never really at home, no matter how eager the people of New York wanted to make him one of them. In Mekas's films there is only one protagonist and one central point of the narrative: Jonas Mekas himself.

The first thing that stands out is what you could call Mekas's messy style. He presents his films as a hodgepodge of images, shakily filmed, shoddily framed, overexposed or out of focus, and wheezily edited in a way that seems more controlled by chance than by dramatic laws. It has been executed so obsessively that it can only be understood as a statement. The camera was not invented for storytelling, the films of Mekas claim, but to document. And maybe not even that. The camera is there for the act of filming: filming is a gesture, and in a way a feat — the filmmaker exists, because he is filming, and what he is filming exists, because he filmed it.

Mekas's cinematic actions are like fleetingly scribbled notes in a diary, although it is questionable whether these notes in a "regular" diary would be found worth writing down. He records in an extreme way the everyday, actions we do not think about, the white noise of our lives — precisely those "events" for which, memory expert Douwe Draaisma says, our memory does not want to make room. Such an event (if we can call it that at all) has not yet taken place, or our memory dismisses it as superfluous to remember.

Mekas prefers to collect those kinds of moments that are already preparing to be forgotten. He seems to be deliberately filming "next to" the topic. They are flashes without centripetal force. Long before the mobile phone freed the camera lens from the eye, Mekas's film camera floated weightlessly through the universe of his life. His fragmentary observations are often too short to really know where you are or to understand who is in the frame. This gives his series of images a curious position in relation to how our memory works.

We remember by telling ourselves stories, by embedding an event from the past in an anecdote or longer narrative in which the dramaturgical laws of novels or film are never far away. Only by forgetting can we turn an event into a story: adding everything together is not a story, but life itself. The story is the handhold of remembering and therefore also the director of forgetting. What does not fit or what stops the story, we exclude, even to the extent that forgetting becomes a form of erasure.

Mekas, on the other hand, tries to transcend these moments or events that could be the anchor points of a story. Mekas collects memories that memory cannot fit into a well-formed story. The moments that are "too much" for memory, the surplus of our lives that is only lived to be immediately forgotten. It is unfair, Mekas suggests, to dismiss this infinite series of small moments from which life is built as too unimportant to remember. With his Bolex, a camera with which he can only shoot a maximum of twenty-five seconds of film each time, he fights against this injustice. Life is made up of a succession of irrelevant incidental events, and he wants to preserve them, even if there is no unity to be found in them or a story to be extracted from, and our memory wants to get rid of them right away. Look, with each of his "wild" shots he holds out to us, isn't life so much more than what we remember of it? So much more than the novel that makes our memory of it?

Yet even Mekas cannot escape the inevitability of the narrative. Whoever puts images together creates an order, even if that order is meant to be chaos. And if the filmmaker or storyteller suggests not wanting to impose order, the viewer or reader does it for him. This urge is so deep within us that I would call it instinctive. If there is something that makes us human, then this is the core of it. Consciousness is about being able to turn life into a story.

When we look at Mekas's series of images, we recognize the rituals of his life, returning people, and personal obsessions, topics that occupy him, temporarily or not. He loves the circus. The ultimate outing is a picnic in the park or by the sea. He loves to film the weddings of his friends. And there are the bigger stories. There is a film about his trip to Lithuania, the reunion with his mother. There is a film about his arrival in the United States, how the Displaced Person becomes a New Yorker. And there's a five-hour film about how he falls in love, gets married, has children. He films his loved ones in his loft, on the street in SoHo or in Central Park, images that we can only understand as home movies, celebrating the happiness of family life. These seem to me to be narratives and to the experienced psychoanalyst that we are as viewers, the "recording" of a life story, an autobiography. In what else could the secret of his life be revealed other than in this narrative, which has been spun out over several films?

Then why did I feel so uncomfortable watching *Reminiscences of a Journey to Lithuania* and *Lost, Lost, Lost (Diaries, Notes and Sketches)*? I think because they were too direct about Lithuania, about Mekas's exile, the history of his flight, and the years as a Displaced Person in Germany, exactly the things Casper had put under tension with his article, the testimonies with which, according to him, Mekas allegedly claimed an undeserved victimhood. I realized that I was resisting taking notes. I didn't want to be the detective looking for evidence, as if I had already made Mekas a suspect.

I looked at them for the first time on a computer screen, where I could freeze them, rewind them, slow them down. I missed the darkness of a cinema in which I could imagine myself unseen, and I missed the empty cinema seat in front of me over which I could lay my legs to surrender to Jonas and his brother's trip to Lithuania or the first impressions of New York in black and white.

It was only after thirty minutes of *Reminiscences* that I made my first and only commentary on that film. It was preceded by sun-drenched images of agricultural machinery working the land of the collective farm of which the family business was now part. This was followed by a richly endowed dinner with mother, brothers and sisters, aunts and uncles, supported by crackling recordings of Lithuanian folk music. Then comes the scene that intrigued me. The family has gathered outside the parental home. They cheerfully compare each other's height. Mekas likes to lose himself in slapstick; he's no different from the average maker of home movies. But then he strikes. Fleetingly and barely noticeable, the nostalgia that lurks beneath the scene reveals itself. In the wooden wall of the farm the heights of his brothers and sisters from their childhood are still engraved. A flash, nothing more. Badly told, the classical dramatist would judge, which Mekas would undoubtedly take as a compliment. With his dragged voice he comments on the scene in a lofty tone: "Oh, these personal ramblings. Of course.

I would like to know about the social realities. How is the life going there in the Soviet Lithuania? But what do I know about it? I am a Displaced Person on my way home in search for my home, retracing bits of past, looking for some recognizable traces of my past. The time in Semeniškiai is being suspended."

The search is personal. Time being suspended. Mekas is not a sociologist, an anthropologist, or a journalist or historian. The trip to Lithuania is a search for what he has forgotten and what he didn't want to forget: the memories as he jotted them down in 1946 in the poems in *Idylls of Semeniškiai*. Now, twenty-five years later, they should not have changed, even though he knows better.

Only after another almost three hours of *Lost, Lost, Lost*, I understand what this means for Mekas. I watch the long closing sequence of the film that is preceded by the title "A visit to Stony Brook." The first part consists of footage shot by his friend Ken Jacobs (also an icon of American experimental film), the second part is shot by Mekas himself. The men are on a day out of town, together with two girlfriends, Barbara [Rubin] and Debbie. The young women insist on swimming in the sea with clothes and all. Mekas films them, Jacobs films the women and the filming Mekas. A glorious autumn day, full of madness and contentment. "It was good, it was good," Mekas sighs on the soundtrack. "All the troubles were washed away by the waters." The women cover themselves with blankets. The car drives on deserted roads. In the back seat, the women dry their hair. They stop to admire a white horse. The sun projects a golden halo on the car windows. Then Mekas switches to the third person in his commentary, as if talking about someone other than himself:

> "Sometimes he didn't know where he was. The present and the past, intermingled, superimposed. And then, since no place was really his, no place was really his home, he had this habit of attaching himself immediately... To any place. He used to joke: 'Oh, drop me in a desert... And come back next week, and you will find me. I'll have my roots deep and wide.' He remembered another day. Ten years ago, he sat on this beach, ten years ago, with other friends. The memories, the memories, again I have memories. I have a memory of this place. I have been here before. I have really been here before. I have seen this water before. Yes, I have walked, upon this beach, these pebbles."

I'm quoting so extensively to show how Mekas reasons. How easily he switches between the general and the concrete, between thoughts and observations, between "he" and "I," and how his memories are tangible to him, touchable, a few pebbles on the beach that are no different from the memory of pebbles ten years earlier. He was here before, but present and past and he and I are not separated by time, they coincide, gliding over each other, blending like the mélange of a fragrant tea.

The reason for this is that he's nowhere at home, "no place is really his." But, I can see, there is a place where he can "come home," in a timeless ("suspended") capsule: his memory. Mekas makes his memories his home, and his camera helps him with that. Not by telling big stories with it, but by capturing the trifles of life. Filming is creating a home, a weightless house that travels with him everywhere, and that nothing or nobody can take away from him.

And then I can't run out of luck – the five hours of *As I Was Moving Ahead Occasionally I Saw Brief Glimpses of Beauty*, Mekas's longest movie and his happiest. One evening, not long before the turn of the millennium, Mekas decides to bring his life from 1972 until then together in one film. He first has tried to figure out the chronology of the film reels that have piled up in his studio, but they are poorly archived, it's a mess. It doesn't matter, he says, what is chronology all about? He'll leave it to chance how this film "develops," the reel his hands find easiest he'll glue to the next one without reflection. "Let it be, let it go," he says on the soundtrack, that's how this film will evolve. They harbor an order of their own. After all, a chronology wouldn't help him to understand his life, or the people around him. He's stopped trying to understand people anyway. Or to understand his own life.

That might sound sad, but Mekas is cheerful, on a constant "high." The prospect of being able to see all those past memories again, all those ephemeralities that every other human being would have forgotten but, thank heavens, captured by him on film, what else can it bring him but a feeling of bliss? For five hours, the pictures of his family life are strung together. Jumping limp, forwards and backwards, an emerging love unrolls, long afternoons in bed, the traces of making love, sunlight peeking along the curtains, a hippie wedding, dinners with friends, drinking wine, mischief of artist-friends, the birth of a daughter, a son, their first steps, picnics in Central Park, meeting friends on the street, premieres in Anthology Archives, unexpected glimpses of Jackie Kennedy. The order is random: falling in love comes after birth, marriage before the long afternoons in bed, suddenly the children are toddlers and then babies, birthdays and birthday cakes, a Christmas dinner... Flickering and flashing, half-framed, out of focus and then sharp, in backlight and overexposed – as a spectator, it's impossible not to be filled with it, addictedly to give in to it, sweet happiness waving in and out of you. Shameless home movies, about shameless bliss, shamelessly served up to be consumed shamelessly.
In between, for no immediate reason, teasing titles, as if Mekas wanted to beat Jean-Luc Godard with a few pastiches.

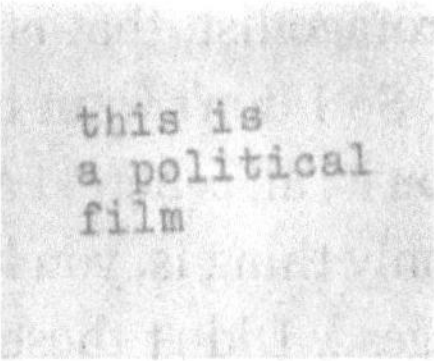

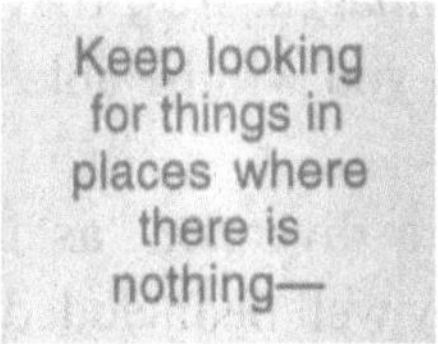

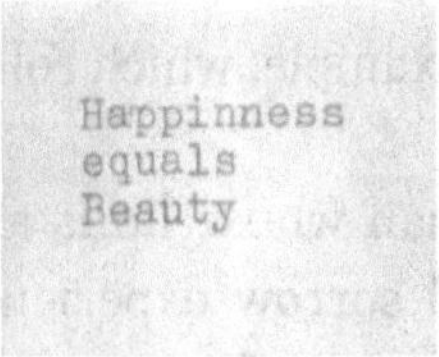

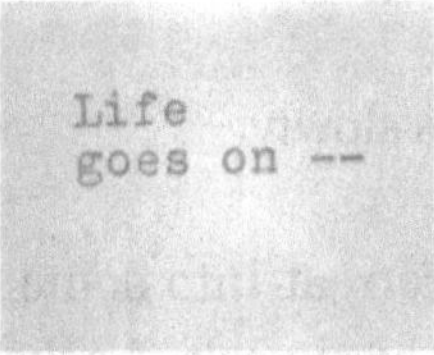

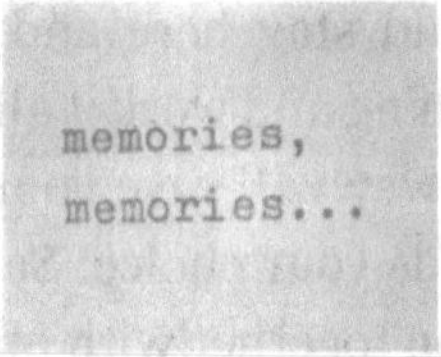

On the soundtrack, he is equally teasing. He jokingly addresses the viewer: "You expect to find out more about the protagonist, that is me, the protagonist of this movie. So I don't want to disappoint you. All I want to tell you is: all is here. I am in every image of this film... the only thing is, you have to know how to read these images... Didn't these French guys tell you how to read images? Yes, they did. Please read these images, and you will be able to tell everything about me."

It seems like a diversion, as I also note a few sentences that may well be included in the psychoanalyst's report.

This title, for example, which rolls slowly by:

> "[...] about a man whose lip is always trembling from pain and sorrow experienced in the past which he only knows–"

Or this one, just as slowly:

> "[...] Should I retreat into some silent place and work it all out by myself, I asked. No, the voice said. You should stay here and continue doing what you are doing and work it all out the difficult way. The easy way will save your soul and a few others. So this is your choice: Salvation by yourself, or salvation together with others–"

Then, we are well into the fifth hour of the film, Mekas suddenly speaks directly to his wife and his children.

Those who provided these images with life with their presence obsessively filmed by their beloved, husband and father. Mekas wonders whether they have the same memories with these images as he does. And then the truth has to come out:

> "I guess I was filming my own memories, my own childhood as I was filming your childhood. I picked up those moments to which I responded, remembering my own childhood. So I don't know how much of yourselves you will see in it. It was all real. It was all real. Life, it's you in every frame of this film. Though it's seen by me, but it is you."

All the time, Mekas filmed his own childhood memories, regaining the paradise of his youth in the life with his wife and children. Nostalgia is at the core of his existence, and filming allowed him to rewrite his own lost childhood. His memory was like a palimpsest. He wrote the new memories over the text of the old ones. For Mekas, filming is regaining lost time in the now, the present of shooting his films. He preserved his own childhood, which he was never able to film, in the pictures of his children.

It moved me. But somewhere it rubbed. Where? There was something that bothered me. Maybe because the story was too beautiful, as if this had been a life without mishaps. Could it? I did some research on the Internet. To Hollis Melton, American poet and Mekas's spouse since 1974, the woman of the lazy afternoons, the mother of their two children, daughter Oona and son Sebastian. Hollis, from whom Mekas was divorced not long before he edited this film, I read.

Divorce? In the five hours of film footage, intertitles, voice overs — nowhere is there even the slightest hint of that word. Mekas had made a five-hour film of family happiness. To cope with his divorce? As if he was circling a black pond, a motionless mirror in which he didn't want to look, a big unsolvable secret that still made him shiver ("a man whose lip is always trembling") and that he only had the courage to see in the eyes by way of a detour? It felt as if a good friend you haven't spoken to for a long time was spending an evening telling you how he had fared, but kept the most important thing from you. What kind of person were you if you could do such a thing?

I remembered a voice-over that I had written down somewhere in the first half hour of the film:

> "Memories, memories: no judgment here, just images and sounds, very innocent in and by themselves, as they pass through as they go and they go. [...] Yes, people are bad, cinema is innocent. Innocent. People are not innocent. They are not."

charisma

After his death on January 23, 2019, in New York, there appeared only one In Memoriam about Mekas in a Dutch publication. Art historian Koen Kleijn, who wrote this fine text for *De Groene* (which can be compared with *The Nation*), later told me that when he first met Mekas in 2010 on a terrace in Vilnius, capital of present-day Lithuania, he had never seen a film by him. The memory of the improvised interview on the spot formed the heart of his I.M. It is indicative of the charisma of the then eighty-seven-year-old Mekas that he needed only a single encounter to charm Koen, which led him back in the Netherlands to read *I Had Nowhere to Go* and Mekas's poems from the forties and fifties. It wasn't until 2017 that Koen was introduced thoroughly to his film oeuvre when curator Adam Szymczyk gave Mekas a major role in Kassel's documenta 14.

I think that many like Koen can tell such a story about Mekas. He charmed countless colleagues, film journalists and celebrities with his lean appearance, his Lithuanian accent when he spoke English, and his ever naughtily twinkling eyes. He was the shy man in the corner of the room everyone wanted to take care of, who, once he spoke, always had an anecdote available or shared his admiration for a film with you. If only he wasn't hiding behind the eyepiece of his Bolex camera, with that rattling sound that his fragile voice couldn't get over. The less he spoke, the more intelligent he seemed. Letting words hang in the air, only to be caught for the good listener, that's what he was good at. And who doesn't want to be the good listener?

I never met Jonas Mekas in person, never physically shook his hand, whereas there were plenty of opportunities for that. My found footage films were screened in programs by Anthology Archives, and during my seven years at the Netherlands Filmmuseum in the 1990s, there were plenty of reasons to collaborate with him. I also have friends and acquaintances who knew Jonas (as he is then invariably called) well. It was also known that without an appointment you could enter Anthology Archives, which retained a certain anarchistic sixties atmosphere, and meet Mekas in his office. Yet there was something about him that kept me from taking action. So much so that, looking back on it, it feels more or less like a deliberate decision. Sometimes it's better not to meet your heroes, I know from experience. Also, with Mekas I was afraid that I was not going to like him. That I would find him too self-centered, especially.

There are moments in his films in which he likes to show off his friendships with celebrities a little too much. Andy Warhol, Yoko Ono and John Lennon, Lou Reed, Jackie Kennedy — they emphatically pass unemphatically, of course out of focus and filmed with a swaying camera, but to me those scenes come across just a little too often as a pedantic find-the-hidden-faces-puzzle: how many celebrities do you recognize in Mekas's everyday life?

Even though Mekas is everywhere with his camera, he wants to be present as casually as possible, as if he isn't actually there. His camera floats among the celebrities, without Mekas bothering about the framing or taking the time to picture them. His style of filming suggests that they are no more important than the blooming cherry blossom in his street, a few raindrops on the window of his loft, the tumbling of one of his children, sunlight radiating the film image. And they're no more important than he is. So why do I feel pride in all those flashy cameos?

In 2003, Mekas released a scrapbook with the postcards he received from his "friends artists" over the years. "It's a sequel to my filmed and written diaries," he writes. A small selection of the names: Joan Crawford, Alan Ginsburg, Patti Smith, Nam Jun Paik, Kenneth Anger, Joseph Cornell, Robert Wilson, Michelangelo Antonioni, Carl Theodor Dreyer, Stan Brakhage, Carl Andre, Bruce Conner, Louise Brooks, Fernand Léger. Didn't he have any "ordinary" people at all as an acquaintance?

It is not only telling that they sent him those often funny and flattering postcards, it is equally telling that Mekas kept them so carefully. It seems as if he needed them to point out to himself that the Lithuanian peasant boy had become someone in that unreachable world. It's the ambiguity of wanting to be unmistakably invisible and at the same time visible: "... me, who was there, even if I wasn't fully there."

The arena in which Mekas sought his way was the milieu of the New York avant-garde and jet set, who, with the rise of Andy Warhol, liked to stay in each other's presence. For the Serpentine Gallery in London, Mekas drew a map in 2014 as he remembered New York in the early 1960s. A broad green line indicates Broadway. Around it he notes places and names that come to his mind. Where Dylan lived, Ornette [Coleman], Oldenburg, La Monte Young, Yoko Ono, [Michael] Snow, [Donald] Judd, Robert Frank, John Cage, [William S.] Burroughs and where Warhol filmed *Sleep*, the Velvet Underground practiced and the famous Vesuvio Bakery was located. No milkman on the corner, no unknown neighbor where he could pick up his key if he had forgotten it, not the newspaper kiosk in his street or the entrance to the subway. His memories weren't that ordinary, which sounds contradictory to the filmmaker of the neglected and the everyday.

Is it strange that I'm only thinking about this now that I'm no longer sure of my admiration? Wouldn't I have had that doubt if I had met Mekas in person? If I had let myself be charmed by him, like Koen? The fact that I only know him from his art, his columns and his interviews, is that different from a personal encounter?

When I asked myself those questions, my first reaction was: Yes, of course. The meeting of two bodies is direct; there is nothing in between. Looking someone in the eye, shaking hands, sensing the smell of cigarette smoke in his clothes, wanting to straighten out his sloppy jacket, seeing a crumb on his chin (and not being able to keep your eyes off it), being overwhelmed by his height, being surprised by his flapping hands or his hard to trace accent — a person who stands in front of you in all his tangibility is immediately knowable (in the sense of "without mediation").

Knowable? That a physical encounter would be more direct is, of course, only an illusion: everyone plays a role, dresses with the signs of it, and behaves according to circumstances. Yet we like to believe in the fiction of direct knowability. If we say that we know someone, the inherent message is that it is his or her physical presence. You have shared a very real space with each other, had a conversation, handed each other a glass.

Michael Casper "knew" Jonas Mekas in this way, which of course in itself gives his historical research a certain tension. He visited Mekas's apartment. They shook hands. Mekas, I imagine, made tea, or poured a glass of wine. They sat at the table, facing each other. Casper looked around curiously, saw the books, folders, fleeting notes on a desk (in which he would like to have a peek), a tiny video camera (which had replaced the Bolex) always within reach. He looked at the hands of Mekas who restlessly wiped imaginary crumbs off the table. He may well have visited the toilet. (Which is a dangerous exercise, I know from experience. Once I interviewed a famous filmmaker in his apartment. I visited his bathroom and was so shocked by the toilet bowl that I hardly dared to go near it. It hadn't been cleaned in weeks. I saw something I didn't really want to know, I realized. I had crossed a boundary of intimacy. I can't think about the films and ideas of this hyper intelligent filmmaker without remembering that toilet.)

Casper could look Mekas in the eye, listen to the intonation of his voice, perceive the stammering in his phrasing, and feel awkward about the knowledge he had brought with him from Lithuania, photocopies of articles from yellowed newspapers, which still showed matters in black and white of which Mekas remembered nothing. He no longer trusted the star of the New York avant-garde who sat opposite him. Mistrust is an unpleasant emotion, which you try to put off for as long as possible. It's something you don't like, but sometimes you have to give in. How do you then behave? How much of that mistrust can you show? There must have been a moment when Casper was thinking: You're showing me a mask, Jonas (I'm sure he could have called him that), but I know that behind all those bullshit stories of yours there's a hidden secret, the memory of an event you don't want to share with me. And if you don't want to share it with anyone, too bad for you, as I will not only reveal that conviction to you, but to the whole world.

It's a scene I'm making up here (it doesn't take much imagination), but I would have liked Casper to tell me what thoughts were playing through his head. In four consecutive emails I asked if I could interview him via Skype. He didn't respond to the idea. He didn't say yes, but neither said no. It irritated me that he ignored my request. Didn't Mekas allow him into his apartment? And if he thought he could put Mekas on the couch of his psychoanalysis, didn't he lose the right to withdraw from it himself? Even if that was for an obscure researcher from a faraway country?

In my opinion, Casper was more than a messenger of an objective historical record. There was a person behind his article; someone who didn't hide the fact that he was annoyed by Mekas's refusal to respond to his questions and doubts. After several excuse emails for the long delay, he finally answered the questions in my first email with carefully formulated but measured answers. Answers that nevertheless sounded honest and candid, which only made me more curious. The whole affair had touched him emotionally.

When I asked him if he had found it difficult to confront Mekas with his research results, he replied:

"Yes, it was uncomfortable to confront Mekas. I lost a lot of sleep over it when I was writing the piece. But it was important for the goals of the piece, and for journalistic integrity, to be transparent with him about what I had found."

Sleepless nights, what does that mean? Uncertainty about his stance? Did he doubt whether he had sufficient proof to lecture Mekas so tenaciously? Or was it painful to "accuse" Mekas, to be his prosecutor? Did he perhaps consider leaving it at that and giving the ninety-five-year-old a quiet old age? Or did he feel obliged to the 2,400 Jewish victims in the forest of Astravas? And was it worth it?

"Study the historian before you begin to study the facts," writes E.H. Carr in his classic study of historiography *What Is History?* A historian brings with him his own past, which interferes with his selections, the paths he takes and the turns he thinks he can skip. Research is never neutral. In the evocative words of E.H. Carr: "The facts are really not at all like fish on the fishmonger's slab. They are like fish swimming about in a vast and sometimes inaccessible ocean; and what the historian catches will depend, partly on chance, but mainly on what part of the ocean he chooses to fish in and what tackle he chooses to use – these two factors being, of course, determined by the kind of fish he wants to catch. By and large, the historian will get the kind of facts he wants."

I'm curious why Casper went fishing in Lithuania

and why he wanted Mekas in his net. A glimpse of his own background, his own biography, might perhaps provide something that remained unsaid in the article. Historians usually show little of themselves, except perhaps in Acknowledgments sections, but while writing the Dutch version of this book I did not manage to get access to his thesis. At the department of Electronic Theses and Dissertations at UCLA, I read that the text of *Strangers and Sojourners: The Politics of Jewish Belonging in Lithuania, 1914–1940* was under embargo until March 21, 2021. At my request as to whether he could send me the digital version, Casper never replied, which I thought strange for an academic. The only reason I can think of is that he intended to publish the thesis in whole or in part at another time, and did not want to pre-release his findings.

There was little left but to scour the Internet, where Casper had scant trace at the time. In 2008 and 2009, he wrote ten stories for *The Forward*, the English language supplement to a Yiddish periodical that has been published in New York since 1897. A critical piece about the Lithuanian carnival and the custom of Lithuanians dressing up as caricatured Jews is striking ("'Jews' Parade on the Streets of Vilna"). In a piece about a rabbi who claims to be a fortune-teller in New York I recognize the "annoyed" and "unmasking" Casper ("A Jewish Mystic Offers Amulets and Predictions, for $180 A Pop"). For *Pakn*

Tregger (a magazine for the Yiddish Bookcenter) in 2016 he translates a novel fragment from *Shtarke un shvakhe* (*The Strong and the Weak*) by photographer and novelist Alter Kacyzne in which the Warsaw of the 1920s is evoked.

The genesis of his thesis can be reconstructed from official press releases with the same, youthful-looking photograph each time (as if he is not getting older; I have found no indication of his age). Casper received a fellowship at The Center for Jewish History in New York City and a residency at the United States Holocaust Memorial Museum, facilitated by The Fund for the Study of the Holocaust in Lithuania Fellow at the Jack, Joseph and Morton Mandel Center for Advanced Holocaust Studies. The latter press release also mentions that he has previously received several academic fellowships, including from the YIVO Institute for Jewish Research, the Association for the Advancement of Baltic Studies, the Center for Jewish History (all three in the United States) and the Posen Society of Fellows (Israel). As of this writing, he is currently a research fellow at the Vidal Sassoon International Center for the Study of Antisemitism, part of The Hebrew University of Jerusalem. An academic career that moves within the triangle of the United States, Lithuania and Israel, in which the Yiddish language and Jewish culture are central.

It is dry information, not comparable with the traces Mekas left behind. Casper must have a Jewish background (I suppose that fits the collaborators of *The Forward* and a magazine of the Yiddish Bookcenter), but I don't know if he has Lithuanian relatives or if he ever lost family in World War II. Why does anyone choose to study the Holocaust? Is there a feeling of responsibility behind his research that goes beyond the desire to build an academic career? Does he write and work for a higher purpose? I can only guess — and that frustrates me. I have the facts Casper presents, but I don't know the historian enough to weigh them.

Unexpectedly for me, after the release of the Dutch version of this essay, a book by Casper is published, co-authored with Nathaniel Deutsch, also a historian of Jewish history. *A Fortress in Brooklyn: Race, Real Estate, and the Making of Hasidic Williamsburg* (2021) is based on ten years of meticulous research into the remarkable history of a group of Holocaust survivors who founded a Jewish Orthodox enclave in Brooklyn's Williamsburg in the 1940s and 1950s. Against all odds, the Satmar sect, originally from Hungary, managed to preserve its insularity in worldly New York. Seemingly contradictory developments in social housing and gentrification went hand in hand: "Rather than an Eastern European shtetl miraculously transported to Brooklyn," Deutsch and Casper write, "the Hasidic enclave in Williamsburg is a distinctly American creation, and its journey from the 1940s to the present is a classic New York City story."

As a reader you get the idea that not one fact of "the most poorly understood two square miles of the United States," as one reviewer described Williamsburg, has escaped their attention. Moreover, Casper and Deutsch know how to put every detail into the relevant sociological and political context. At the same time, they describe the events as if they have no personal connection to them: not a word about where their fascination with this "exotic Jewry" comes from, not even in an introduction or in the extensive "Acknowledgments," which concludes with "[...] we are especially grateful to the numerous Hasidim who shared their time and knowledge with us in the homes, *shtiblekh*, and streets of Williamsburg." From an interview with *The Forward*, I learn that Casper and Deutsch at some point have both lived in or near Williamsburg. They do not grant the reader of their book a glimpse of it. They present their findings in a strictly objectified way. They place themselves as that strange, impersonal god of classical, scientific historiography outside the text. To those who, at the suggestion of E.H. Carr, want to get to know them first, they offer nothing.

In Casper's dissertation *Strangers and Sojourners*, which I am finally able to download in March 2021, it is not different. The same objectified tone. The same detailed exposé. And nowhere the sense of place where it all happened, or the dust of the archival records. Casper chronicles in *Strangers and Sojourners* how

Jewish intellectuals between 1914 and 1940 sought to build themselves into the new project of an increasingly nationalized concept of "Lithuania" to secure the protections extended to the Jewish community in the 14th century. During the first years of independence after World War I they sound still optimistic. Starting in 1926, under the authoritarian (proto-fascist) regime of Antanas Smetona, they grow more cautious. They debate what they saw as the justifiable desire for relative autonomy for the Jewish minority, harking back to the unique position of the Jews in the medieval Grand Duchy of Lithuania (Grand Duke Vytautas the Great granted far-reaching privileges to the Jews in 1388, one of those moments in the Jewish diaspora that is written in golden letters). From 1926 on, there is more pragmatic reasoning and political bargaining when Smetona suggests that he will leave the Jewish minority alone if they also show him peace. Which is not to say that the dictator in the 1930s seeks to neutralize the anti-Semitism of his former prime minister Augustinas Voldemaras and his "Iron Wolves" (also known as the "Lithuanian Ku Klux Klan"), as the Jews are too easy a scapegoat for economic recession.

I can't manage to read the dissertation without having my stomach in knots. Not because Casper presents the history of the Jewish community in Lithuania between 1914 and 1940 as an apocalypse in the making. On the contrary. "While there is no doubt that Lithuania had its share of political disappointments and anti-Semitism," Casper writes, "I try here to resist 'backshadowing', or writing teleologically, and seek instead to frame events, as much as possible, in their immediate historical context." Casper's objectifying tone makes you feel all the more acutely that these Jewish intellectuals are living and debating in a present that they may be experiencing as grim, but without being able to imagine what unfathomable definition that word in the near future will be given. And that is precisely what makes reading this history unbearable. For as a reader, you do know what horror is looming over these inspired, hopeful thinkers, who are doing everything they can to make it clear that they *belong* in Lithuania.

It is quite possible that Casper doesn't consider my tinkering in his own background relevant. He presents the facts, what can be "personal" about that? At the same time, I can't believe he's naive. He knows Mekas's film work well, and he also recognizes the more philosophical consequences of it. Moreover, the tone of his article in the *NYRB* is literary; the article is composed in a virtuoso way, in which I spot the hand of an essayist rather than that of a pure historian. However, the article seems to be an exception. Casper is visible in it in a way that he does not allow himself to be in his other work — nor to the questioning writer from far away Holland.

*

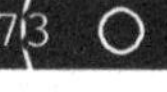

Where am I in this great story of the Holocaust? On the sidelines, far beyond the sidelines even, which has become an uncomfortable position in the current tendency around identity politics and the ideas about the "right to speak" that go with it. I have no Jewish background. I learn from the Internet that Vianen, the birthplace of my two parents, had eight Jewish residents during the Second World War. Two of them recently were honored with so-called "stumbling stones" in the pavement in front of their house at the time. They commemorate the couple Moses and Alberdina Salomon-Van Zwanenberg. They lived at the end of the street where I was born thirteen years after their deportation, 200 meters from my mother's family home and 400 meters from the house where my father lived all his life and my mother moved in when they were married. My parents' stories about the war revolved around curfew, blackout, food stamps, listening to Radio Orange illegally, going into hiding to escape forced labor, stealing butter from a German truck, confiscated bicycles and wooden tires, interned German soldiers, the air raid on the bridge over the river and the death of a careless or overconfident (depending on the narrator) resistance fighter, killed on the run near the old city wall. There were no Jews in those stories, not even the Salomons and their tragic end in Auschwitz, nor the forced sale of their orchard.

There was only one Jew my father could vividly tell about, even if it was a story that took place after the war. The writer Herman de Man (mainly known for his novel *The Rising Water*) had been a friend my grandfather's family for the few years he had lived in Vianen. Maybe the word "family friend" was too strong. He joined the parish priests and chaplains who liked to visit my grandfather on Sunday afternoons to smoke cigars. My father was still a kid then. De Man, who was actually called Sal Hamburger, had converted to the Roman Catholic faith in the early twenties, which no one had missed in the small town. His wife and he were baptized in the parish church and the widely publishing intellectual was "welcomed" by the Catholic notables, of which my grandfather was one.

He did not stay long in Vianen, which he would later characterize as "rigid as a stiff, ugly gentlewoman." After Ina Boudier-Bakker (who lived across the street from my grandfather's house), he was the second writer who ruthlessly scolded the petty bourgeois inhabitants of the small provincial town. My mother must have recognized this: she hated the sprawl of gossip and backbiting, the housewives chatting in the street to share the latest "novelties."

When the war broke out, the De Mans family lived in Berlicum (situated in a southern province of the Netherlands). However, he was in France to work on a new novel and escape his bad marriage. He did not return to the Netherlands, eventually fled to England, where he worked for Radio Orange, and then left for Curaçao. There he awaited the end of the war.

When he returned to the Netherlands, he had to discover that the Nazis in Auschwitz had murdered his wife and four of their six children, as well as his father, brother and sister-in-law. Dutch policemen who had a strange idea of duty had delivered his wife and children to Camp Vught. The mayor of Berlicum had made no attempt to warn them of approaching fate; four precious hours to flee had been lost. The fury about this consumed De Man, a fire raged inside him, a man who was already known for his tempestuous nature.

In that mood, he visited Vianen and the family home of my father, who by now was twenty-nine years old. My father could reenact the scene as if he were Marlon Brando. De Man pulled himself up by the banister of the stairs with both hands. His voice barked and moaned, his eyes wide open, his face distorted in pain. He was a broken man, inconsolable and craving revenge. The Dutch had allowed his wife and children to be murdered. They had even cooperated. The way my father portrayed it, it was a mixture of despair and anger. The stairs were still the same as where the event had actually taken place.

The story didn't go any further than this scene. Maybe the rest wasn't so easy to reenact. I find it difficult to put comforting words in my grandfather and father's mouths, as I have no idea if they had any. It's remarkable enough that De Man visited them, so soon after the horrible news about his family. In any case, my grandfather did not show him the door, which happened to many who returned from the camps.

It was only later that I understood the far larger story behind this anecdote. And it is only now that I realize that my parents saw no reason to start talking about the Salomon-Van Zwanenberg couple, and the empty house they had left in our street. How often on Sunday afternoon walks or on our way to a day on the beach at the river did we not pass that spot?

Does that deprive me of the right to lecture Mekas? Or to judge Casper if he thinks he has the right to accuse Mekas?

Some forty years ago, I visited Auschwitz, twenty-two years old (Mekas's war age). I was on vacation with a friend and we traveled through Poland, which at the time was still behind the Iron Curtain. My friend stayed in the car, he didn't feel the need for a visit. It is difficult to recall the pure memory of what I saw and felt then, because too many films and television programs and books have filled it up. However, writing about it now brings back the silence of the place. The paths were muddy. I respectfully strolled past the cabinets with suitcases, coats, shoes, hair, and toys. It seemed to me details for poetic contemplations; I considered the possibilities for a poem, clinging to an incomprehensible suffering. Sufferings, I realize now, of which I did not see the unfathomable at all, as my mind was too young for that. Appearances, clichés, nothing deep or penetrating. I was in a place that would sound like somewhere important if I told someone I had been there. I don't feel like pretending this to be any better than it comes back to me now.

Maybe it's the comment of the friend who stayed behind in the car that hangs over it. He labeled my interest as false sentiment. I wouldn't help the victims by entering the barracks, gas chambers and ovens. What he was trying to say was that I went there to feel good, to indulge in my own tribute, without really feeling anything for the people who had been gassed, tortured or starved to death. You don't need that place for that, he believed. In fact, you desecrated the place, with which he predicted how Auschwitz would become a tourist attraction, as Sergei Loznitsa recorded in all its ambiguity for the former concentration camps Dachau and Sachsenhausen in his 2016 documentary titled after the W.G. Sebald novel, *Austerlitz*.

Still, I am happy with the memory, precisely because the visit was complimented with the stories, films and books that came later. They have given meaning to the place, afterwards and over many years. Meaning that would have faded much more easily without that linkage in my memory, without the concreteness of the place and the footprint I left behind. I could imagine the bleakness of evil, the industrialization of mass murder, the people who belonged to those shoes, and the apparent innocence of the morning light playing in the smoke and mist.

d i a r y

Mekas's films are usually called diary films. It suggests a glimpse into his personal life, and an intimacy that most filmmakers don't give in to. It's true, of course, that everything in Mekas's work revolves around Jonas; at the same time, his films create distance through their form. The swinging camera, the blurred shots, the overexposures, the short length of each shot, and the unconventional framing, it gets on many spectators' nerves.

Mekas's diary films evoke a general feeling of "being there" rather than actually allowing the viewer into the (inner) world of Mekas: "... me, who was there, even if I wasn't fully there." Whoever wants to give in to it, ends up in a state of intoxication, a free-floating mood: you have to allow yourself to get lost in a disorderly memory. Those who want to know at any moment where they are and why, drop out.

Filming, other than writing, suggests a public intention from the moment of recording. Even the most intimate home movies are made to be watched later with others. They are different from a diary in which the writer initially writes for himself. A private world, a conversation with yourself, sharing secrets with the silent, attentive paper — these are the qualities we attribute to a diary.

For those who want to get to know Mekas, looking for his secret self without having to shake his hand, his written diaries seem to be the best source. Casper too, I suspect, was expecting direct access to Mekas's inner world.

In the introduction to *I Had Nowhere to Go*, the diaries published in 1991 that Mekas had kept in Germany and New York between 1944 and 1955, he reveals something that, in the light of Casper's article, immediately sounds ominous: "As I reread these diaries I do not know anymore, is this truth or fiction. It all comes back again, with the vividness of a bad dream that makes you jump up in bed all trembling; I am reading this not as my own life but someone else's, as if these miseries were never my own. How could I have survived it? This must be someone else I am reading about."

Mekas describes an emotion that is recognizable to each of us. We only have to see a photo of our younger self. We appear to ourselves as a stranger. But now that the historical checker and judge is joining me (Casper's eyes are everywhere by now), I suddenly read Mekas's observation as a form of covering-up, as if he doesn't want to vouch for the words of his younger self, pulls his hands off him.

Of course, he didn't mean it that way when he wrote it. Mekas was still in the days of innocence. He imagined his younger self not being watched over. Yet with what at first seems to be a literary trick, Mekas set something in motion that ironically enough could turn against him many years later. By distancing himself, he presented the diary as a document. It became a found object, the shards of an archaeological excavation stuck together. As a result, and which indeed feels paradoxical, it gained in truth. Time has passed over these texts, Mekas pointed out, so much so that it has become history, an archive of experiences of someone we can no longer really know or meet, but have to take his word for it. The diary became a historical document, which Mekas did not have to take responsibility for in 1991.

From the moment that Casper appears on stage, another twenty-five years or so later, the older Mekas is suddenly expected to be held accountable for this document of that young man who is "a stranger" to him. The words of yesteryear have gained new weight. These are the very words of Jonas Mekas, says the historian. Young or old, they come from the same body, and the old body will have to vouch for what the young man has written, or in this special case has not written or has written in veiled form.

But to which history do Mekas's words belong? For there is a complication. After all, there are only two passages in *I Had Nowhere to Go* that are of interest to Casper as historical evidence. Only they don't come out of the diary! They come from the introduction, which means they are memories from 1991. They are not written down immediately after the events, and they are not memories that are still "fresh" in the mind. Which raises the question: Do they have the same credibility as the diary? And is the Mekas from 2018 more accountable for the memories of 1991, when he was sixty-nine years old, than for the (almost directly written down) memories from 1944, when he was still at the youthful age of twenty-two?

Right from the first paragraph of the introduction, Mekas provides the information that interests Casper. And me no less, since I have become — at least temporarily — his accomplice. Mekas was twenty-two years old, he relates, when he embarked on a journey that finally brought him from the small Lithuanian village of his birth to New York: "I was a young man of some reputation. For over a year, I had worked as editor-in-chief of a provincial weekly paper. I had worked as the technical editor of a national semi-literary weekly for another year." It states it in black and white, not a hint of shame. On the contrary, Mekas remembers his young self as someone with "a certain reputation" in rather important positions with two weekly newspapers.

Mekas doesn't say a word about what you could read in the two magazines, but there's nothing suggesting he might have the slightest idea he has something to hide. In his recollection there is only the pride about the young man who has maneuvered himself into two respectful positions with heavy responsibilities. If the sixty-nine-year-old presents these two jobs for any reason, then as a signal that even his younger self, who appears to him as a "stranger," was not lacking in talents that later, when he edits the legendary *Film Culture*, came in very handy to him. And I can't help but get the impression that this strange young man isn't so strange to him at all. On the contrary, he seems genuinely proud that he was once housed in his body. There is no reason to distance himself from him.

It's just that some twenty-five years later Casper travels to Lithuania and browses those newspapers. Might he have feared something? As a historian of Judaism and Jewish belonging in Lithuania he knows the reputation of the newspapers and magazines that appeared during the Second World War. But only if you actually browse them can you ascertain the truth. This is how historical archive research works: seeing and reading with one's own eyes.

If Mekas, as he writes in the introduction to *I Had Nowhere to Go,* was "editor-in-chief" and "technical editor," then he was responsible for publishing anti-Semitic articles calling for the extermination of his Jewish fellow citizens. Articles he did not write himself. But what does an editor-in-chief do other than collect articles and approve them for publication?

For me, it raises different, less rhetorical questions.

Why doesn't Mekas make any effort to conceal his role in those periodicals? Does he assume that no one will read them again? Or did he indeed not realize what he had published? And in the light of the Holocaust this would certainly be blamed on him? Or did his memory leave him in the dark and did he simply forget those anti-Semitic articles? Disinterest only becomes an unpleasant trait when you're reminded of it. Most of the time, no one notices. Until the boomerang returns.

Strangely enough, Casper never refers to the masthead of the newspaper. Wouldn't the "corroborating fact" of Mekas's position be found there? And does this mean that Mekas's name and/or function is not mentioned at all? Was his role indeed perhaps less important than he presented himself to have had?

It doesn't matter much to Casper. In the introduction to *I Had Nowhere to Go*, he reads a confession. It states in black and white which positions Mekas held with those magazines. Doesn't jurisdiction also consider the confession to be the queen of evidence? Believing someone who accuses himself – for judges as well as historians, there's often no other option. Casper believes the confession. It's his only hold. Mekas has written it down in full sanity. Without coercion or the fierce lamp with which an interrogator blinds him.

The second passage revolves around the story of the flight. An event that took place in 1944 and which

Mekas wrote down in 1991. There are, I repeat once more, forty-seven years in between. During the occupation of Lithuania by the Germans, Mekas typed out BBC messages for an underground newspaper. The Germans knew the typeface and tried to trace the publisher through the typewriter. That's why Mekas hid it under a pile of firewood behind the house after each use. One night he discovered that the typewriter had been stolen. If it would fall into the hands of the Germans via the thief, the latter would certainly betray him in order to save his own skin. Mekas, so his friends in the underground believe, must "disappear."

There are two possibilities. He can join the communist partisans or the nationalist. Mekas has his doubts about both. The communists supported by the Soviet Union would not accept him, as he once published an anti-Stalin poem — the Soviets were not reputed for their forgetfulness, nor for their forgiveness. Joining the nationalists is equally unattractive. Then too, the advancing Soviet troops would see him as a collaborator and an enemy of the people. Their cheering welcome of the Nazis in 1941 was difficult to forget or forgive, even though they had later turned against the Germans.

An uncle had a better idea. He had contacts in Vienna, and Jonas and his brother should go there to university. The uncle produced papers that would allow them to travel as students. Then the diary begins: July 19, 1944. Two days later the brothers realize that they can forget about Vienna. They are arrested and forced to work in Hamburg. The "students" have become "forced laborers."

Casper mentions the story of the typewriter, but doubts whether this was the real reason for the flight. The Red Army is advancing upon the Lithuanian border and may march in at any moment. Lithuanians who leave for Germany in the same days are almost all on the run from the Soviets, a renowned Lithuanian historian confirms for Casper. In addition, he doubts the scheme of the flight: to study in Vienna with false papers in order to prevent a possible unmasking by the Germans as a member of the underground. Vienna was under siege by the Allies at that time. The word that comes to hang above the story of the flight is "improbable."

The first sentence of the diary reads: "Today our train pulled into Dirschau, near Danzig. This is our eighth day on the road." An observation, which immediately sounds different from a memory that has been passed by the years. The second paragraph is of a different order: "I am neither a soldier nor a partisan. I am neither physically nor mentally fit for such life. I am a poet."

These two paragraphs immediately bring together the two registers of the diary. First of all, it is a record of actual events: now we are here, now there, now we eat this, now we are hungry, now we are fleeing from Allied bombings, now from the Germans, now we are buying bicycles and we are leaving, now we are waiting for trains that do not come, now we are stuck in trains that do come, now we have found a table in front of our barracks and now we are reading this book and after that this other one — books are the most recurrent theme in the "events." Next to it or across it are the contemplations, the mental processing of events, in which one theme dominates: homesickness. Here, too, the emotions are "fresh," and certainly not consistent, because day after day the mood can change, from hope to despair, from brief satisfaction to annoyance, from hope to disillusionment.

In the diary, we're there. It's driven by the chronology of life, and there's little consistency in that, because that's not how life works. Only in our memory does this fickle chronology become a story, is it rubbed into a narrative with a beginning, a middle and an end. Not much else than under the pressure of an interrogation, of which the report of the offense is the result. Also these reports written to give a lifelike sequence of often fatal events impose the consistency of a story, told with a dramatic coherence, which, not unimportantly, is the beginning of a lot of tunnel vision in police investigation. Both our memory and an official report make events readable, and the novel or short story is the model. And any writer can tell you that omitting is the secret of good storytelling.

Which of the two is more truthful, the diary, and thus the fickle chronology of life, or the novel in our memory, in which the report is streamlined and a dramatic conclusion is worked towards, whereby the laws of suspense and fierce twists help us to remember the story? I notice that I rate the veracity of the diary higher than that of the memory. The directness of the diary is overwhelming. But it also puzzles me.

It is difficult to digest the jumble of events and contemplations in Mekas's diary. It simply refuses to become a story. The twists and turns are too much caused by coincidence. I'm waiting for conclusions that don't come. I read a feuilleton of which the writer doesn't know the end yet, not even what awaits him the next day. A novel is a retrospective, a past tense summary. A diary is the expression of a flowing present, with each day an open ending. Our memory is a novel. Life is a diary.

And there is a further paradox: in the end I can only get a grip on the diary by making a story out of it myself. By extracting thematic threads, searching for the really important twists and turns (in my eyes!), and reading it as the travel story Mekas promised in his introduction: how did this young man from Lithuania end up in New York? But when Mekas wrote the passages that divide this journey into stages for me there was no mention of New York, or of the man (again "of a certain reputation") that he would become there.

How differently I read in the introduction the memory of the flight story from Lithuania, written in

1991. It is served as an anecdote, stored in Mekas's memory as a completed story, polished by time. Not at all surprising, because it's not the first time he's told this story. I also knew it from *Reminiscences of a Journey to Lithuania*, the film about his visit to his motherland in August 1971, twenty-seven years after his flight from Lithuania. In almost identical wording. The story has already proved its merit (perhaps also at the dinner table with family or friends) and doesn't have the precariousness of a diary fragment. In fact, in 1991 it reads like a self-assured prelude to the publication of the diary. The flight is the beginning of a journey that we, the readers, already know where it will end. The chaos of the diary is swept away with it. The diary may be a messy narrative, but we don't have to worry about the end: a new life in New York – and what a life.

There's something else about the flight story. In 1971, Mekas is then forty-nine years old, it is in *Reminiscences of a Journey to Lithuania* the most important hinge of his life story. There is a before and an after. When he tells about it, it is not because of alleged heroism, but as the most painful moment in his life: forced to leave Lithuania behind, lose his "home" and never to be without homesickness again.

Mekas's life was once broken into two pieces. The war is to blame. But it is not the events of the first four years of the war that, according to his memory, decisively marked his later life. The major trauma, the unhealed injury, is not to be found there. The departure from Lithuania caused the pain, and because memory is very good at preserving mental pain, this is the recurring event. As a memory and as a story that has to be told over and over again.

His life in New York may be read as a success story, but the years that preceded it, first as a Displaced Person in Germany, then in poverty-stricken conditions in the United States, definitely colored the flight as a trauma. If Mekas feels like a victim of Communists or Nazis, of Soviets or Germans, then not because of what happened in the first years of the war, but because of the forced farewell in 1944 of Semeniškės, his father and mother, brothers and sister. Homesickness is his pain, even when his later life seems so happy.

That is the underlying novel I recognize in *Reminiscences of a Journey to Lithuania* and *I Had Nowhere to Go*. The war is a big gap in that story, which is hardly filled in. It is typical that the diary in *I Had Nowhere to Go* begins eight days after his flight from Lithuania. Mekas destroyed the diaries he kept before that date even before he left Lithuania, because, he says, his frankness about both the crimes of the Soviets and those of the Nazis could endanger him.

July 21, 1944, the second day on which Mekas writes in his diary, begins like this: "Good-bye, Vienna! At least temporarily. Oh, how naive we were! Even after all these years of war, we haven't really understood yet that THIS IS REALLY WAR." In July 1944, that sounds different than if it had been written in 1991. It sounds authentic. The years may have flown by, it was war, but was it really "war" in Semeniškiai and Biržai – apart from that horrible, forgotten day, when 2,400 Jews were murdered?

The victimhood cherished by Mekas does not lie in the war. Although the diary begins in the last year of the war, these contemplations too are dominated by being "displaced," being chased away from home. It is as if Mekas, consciously or unconsciously, has put those first years of war at the bottom of his list of priorities. Right away, back in 1944.

Or did he want to invoke his right to remain silent from the outset about those "suspect" years of war? Casper will find little in the diary section of *I Had Nowhere to Go* for Mekas's indictment. Is that why he focused his arrows on the escape story in the introduction? He has Mekas's recollection of it from 1972 and repeated in 1991. A story he does not consider trustworthy. Too succinctly told, he suggests; the intentions aren't fairly described. For Casper, it is nothing else than a cheap flight; the underlying motives are less high profile than Mekas wants them to appear. Mekas fears the Soviets, because he has worked for the nationalist magazines. But Casper has no confession in his hands. That's why he dismisses the escape story as a smokescreen. He's trying to undermine its credibility.

Which causes an odd paradox. Where Casper takes "editor-in-chief" and "technical editor" from the introduction as an irrefutable confession, he reads the escape story from the same introduction as a false confession. He adds up two things that he values in opposition to each other differently. A truth and a lie constitute together the basis of his doubt.

I browse through my copy of *I Had Nowhere to Go*, which I didn't read before Casper's article was published. I reread my highlighted passages. They are mainly observations that have acquired meaning in the light of Casper's reasoning. Once again I'm a detective at a crime scene where I'd rather not want to be. I have Mekas on my couch and will deflate him, alert for unconscious confessions and meaningful slips of the tongue. It will come as no surprise that these passages are all about memories.

On September 3, 1947, Mekas wonders why he barely remembers anything about *La belle et la bête*, Jean Cocteau's film that he saw shortly before, when he does remember the heat of the day when they crossed the Rhine to go to the cinema: "Everything that I see, or read, or listen to, connects, translates into moods, bits of surroundings, colors. No, I am not a novelist. No precision of observation, detail. With me everything is mood, mood, or else — simply nothingness."

That same day he attends a lecture on Pirandello, which makes him muse about the memories that really occupy him. Memories of his parents' farm and his childhood: "That's what I am thinking about. I remember a lot of things that are of no use to anybody. They keep coming back to me." He remembers a thousand songs he learned in his native village: "Their words and melodies are in the deepest atoms of my body."

Christmas Day 1948, Mekas is once again filled with nostalgia. A sentence comes to mind by the Lithuanian poet Kossu whom he read at home, under the light of a kerosene lamp, his mother at the spinning wheel, the wool slipping through her hands, the reassuring hum of the spools. "Ah, how beautiful you are from afar!" Kossu versed. He read that sentence, but didn't understand it. Yet it stuck in his memory like a thorn. Only now does he understand this sentence, as well as his recollections of all the little noises around the house, the creaking of the snow, the shadows on the wall, the smell of freshly baked bread, the sound of a sledge outdoors, the horse's hooves, the cracking ice in the river. Sweet memories that overgrow the reminiscence of the hard work; the loneliness during the herding of the cattle; his rough hands about which the schoolchildren in the city teased him. Memories that he only now experiences as sweet, now that he is so far away from where they took place: "Why did I need all this misery, and the life of an exile, a Displaced Person, to understand all this, to feel them with my whole being, my body, those few words, those simple words written by another poet, in another exile, many years ago."

Memories, he can't get away from them. In the undated closing passages from 1955, Mekas complains that these memories keep haunting him: "I always wanted to go forward. I tried to forget everything. But every little detail remained stuck sharply inside. And now they burn. [...] These voices of my past, they creep into my ears, they float in the air, they enclose me tighter and tighter." So, not all recollections are sweet. In fact, they haunt Mekas, harrowing his memory, which can't shake them. He yearns for a rigorous forgetting, to not have to listen to all those voices from the past: "It seems to me that the only direction of my life is always forward. From fear that the past may catch up with me."

Mekas never specifically indicates which memories he wants to avoid. But what is clear is that if he wants to be grounded in New York, if he wants to make his new home there, he has to erase the old home, forget it. New York has to supply a new set of memories. Why is that so hard? Overlooking a lake in New England he sees himself with his mother walking through the fields, his little hand firmly in hers: "... and the field was burning with red and yellow flowers, and I could feel everything like then and there, every smell and color and the blue sky ... I was sitting there and trembling with memory."

Fleeing from memories that can't be shoved away. They intrude, even at an innocent glance of a sun-drenched lake in New England. The flight is without end. Remembering is painful, even sweet recollections, because it brings Mekas to where he would like to be, but cannot go.

Casper believes he knows which memories Mekas is trying to avoid. Those of the Jews of Biržai, although he needs the scrutiny of close reading to identify a passage in which Mekas "betrays" himself.

On February 15, 1948, Mekas writes that he cannot sleep. He wanders through the barracks, observing the moonlight falling on his bed. He remembers the walk he had taken the previous day in the forest of Wilhelmshöhe, a place, he confesses, where he would rather not go. The forest frightens him. Nature evokes too many memories: "The slightest movement of the dark surface of the pond, the rotten, putrid black leaves on the bottom, the willow trees leaning and dipping their branches into the water, the steep banks — everything is calling me back, waking up the memories of Astravas and Biržai."

It's a passage I know from Casper's article (and I already quoted it), but only when I read it again did I realize that nothing came after that. Those who don't know what happened in the forest of Astravas, that in a single day 2,400 Jews were murdered and buried there, are completely in the dark about what Mekas refers to.

This, of course, did not apply to Mekas himself. If he knew what kind of horror he unveiled to his diary in that sleepless night, the reader of the published diaries wouldn't have a clue. That makes the passage a testimonial without substance, nothing more than the representation of a "mood." Even if publishing the diary suggests openness, it doesn't give in to it. In the only moment in his diary that he perhaps has spoken about the Jews of Biržai, they are not openly mentioned.

The silent, listening paper did not contradict Mekas. It only received what he wished to entrust to it. At the time of writing, this was possibly an unbearable honesty. But at the time of typing it out and translating it for publication, it was at least half-hearted. If Casper hadn't told me what took place in the forest of Astravas, I would never have been able to guess what was underneath this passage. Or, to be more precise, what *could be* hidden underneath it.

Does that make the publication of the diaries gratuitous? Does it suggest a sincerity that isn't there, a frankness without consequences? Does that one passage shed a different light on all the other 469 pages?

I have never kept a diary myself, which is probably why I looked at that of Mekas with a naive eye. Diaries have always appeared to me to be a goldmine for biographers; the most authentic document you can get from a person. Where can the biographer get closer to his subject than precisely in these "fresh" memories, usually no more than a day old, sometimes even shorter? And where would the writer be more honest than exactly in these secluded pages? Remembering the little lock on my older sister's colorful diary, which could only be opened with a golden key, will certainly have contributed to this impression.

While researching this essay, I told a brother-in-law at a dinner party what I was working on. When I mentioned Mekas's diary, he immediately jumped to the subject. Just the week before, he had been reading an old diary of his own. There was a passage that still puzzled him. During his student days in Nijmegen he visited a student society in Leiden. During the outward voyage, a draw was made for who had to make a speech on behalf of their delegation. My brother-in-law drew the straw. The speech was not a success, he said, not to say disappointing. His performance was a failure. The memory was still clear to him. In the diary, however, he read something completely different. His performance had just gone well. He had done his job very skillfully and on behalf of his society he had addressed the students of Leiden glowingly. That account, written a day later in his diary, was not correct. It said the opposite of what had really happened. "The weird thing," he said, "is that I do remember the event, but not that I lied about it in my diary."

However, the story went even further. Next to the disputed passage was a question mark in pencil, very thin and delicate. And this presented him with an even bigger riddle. When did he put that question mark there? He did not remember. And he hadn't reread his old diaries so often in his life. The funny thing was that my brother-in-law was more worried about that question mark (the how and why and when), than about the lie.

I still got carried away with the lie, because for whom would he have put it there? For his later I, who would read it again years later? To be able to look back with satisfaction on an event of which he would have forgotten the true facts? Could you be so sneaky with memories that you manipulated them even before they became real memories? Or did he write for readers other than himself, readers he might not even know, but on whom he still wanted to make a good impression? Did he assume at all that he could forget the lie? Didn't he realize that our failures carve more sharply into our souls than our successes? And then that cautious question mark, not a simple "no" on the margin, or a cross, but a sign of hesitation, skepticism perhaps, while now, much later, he was quite sure how this painful event had unfolded.

There was, of course, another possibility. The speech had indeed taken place as described in the diary, but the memory of my brother-in-law had started to gnaw at it. Maybe his later I couldn't imagine that his young I could have withheld so glowingly. The event may have been infected by later disappointments, so that the representation in the diary suddenly appeared as a lie. That would explain the hesitant question mark. When

I presented that possibility to my brother-in-law, he resolutely rejected it. He knew well enough that speeches had never been one of his talents. No, no, no, he said unexpectedly fiercely, his memory was correct, not the diary's representation.

I asked the other dinner guests for their opinion. The diary writers among them assured me that if I ever saw their diaries, I shouldn't believe them blindly. Someone said that in her diary, she often wrote how she had wished for certain events. She also wrote irregularly, often driven by infatuation or heartbreak, but what had happened between those two states of mind, I wouldn't find in it. What was more remarkable was that all the diarists at the table agreed that a diary would be a very unreliable source for finding out what had really happened in their lives. At most, it was a document in which you could read back their moods, but for the facts I really had to look elsewhere.

oral history

It is telling that for the life Jonas Mekas has led, there is so much material available to "get to know" him. Mekas himself is in charge of most of it. He has condensed his life in Lithuania into nostalgic anecdotes. Casper wanted to know what really happened and started questioning him. He presented Mekas with facts he didn't remember. Or that Mekas provided with a different interpretation.

I tried to imagine how such a meeting had been, without realizing that there was a treasure waiting for me that would bring me very close to it. It took a while before the Google algorithms understood what I was looking for, but in the end it appeared as a self-evident item in my search results. There existed an oral history interview that Mekas had done for the United States Holocaust Memorial Museum (USHMM). One of the nine thousand personal testimonies that the museum has collected about the run-up to and the genocide during the Second World War. Two sessions, one of four hours and one of two. Six hours of Mekas in his own words: about his youth and the war years in Biržai, more detailed and in-depth than he had ever been in his films or publications about this period. To be found online from front to back. There was only one complication: the interview was recorded after the publication of Casper's article.

The first session on June 29, 2018, took place just three weeks after the publication date of *The New York Review of Books*. Which is painfully palpable. Mekas looks fragile and insecure. He stutters and has trouble finding the right words, which is not the best way to be convincing. The English language seems to be his enemy, as if he has never been further from home than in those last months of his life. At the end of the second session, two days later, Lithuanian words pour out of his mouth. He never abandoned that language, I realized. Or has Lithuania never left him?

Interviewer Ina Navazelskis tries with iron patience to keep Mekas on the trail of his memories. She is the empathic listener he needs more than ever at that moment. For a "pure" oral history interview, Casper actually gets in her way. More than once Mekas is on the defensive against an absent opponent. He mangles Casper's name, or calls him "that guy," "my friend," or "Michael." Navazelskis, who is interviewing for posterity, repeatedly adds "Casper" and mentions the article as neutrally as possible, although she would rather keep that actuality out of Mekas's story. She wants to know what happened "then" and not what is happening "now." For Mekas, it is "that dirty piece" that troubles him: "You must be aware that somebody did a very, sort of dirty paper on me..."

I'm beginning to wonder if Mekas himself has pressed for the interview, and saw an opportunity for a rebuttal in it. In a conversation via Skype, Navazelskis tells me that it has gone very differently. Mekas has been on the museum's list since 1972, after the release of *Reminiscences of a Journey to Lithuania*. Her predecessor tried for years to convince him to cooperate, but he put it off. The same applied to his brother Adolfas, also a filmmaker and for many decades a film teacher at the renowned Bard College.

In 2011, Adolfas finally promises an interview with Navazelskis, but he wants to wait until he has undergone hospital treatment. He dies on his sickbed, and the interview never takes place.

Navazelskis's cameraman is acquainted with Jonas and suggests trying to convince him one more time. Together they visit a poetry night in Brooklyn where Mekas performs and afterwards they talk with him. To their surprise, he agrees. He suggests a date somewhere at the end of June. Two weeks after the encounter, Casper's article is published. Navazelskis had no idea this was in the planning. The appointment goes through, and she meets a broken man. "Mekas was very hurt and bewildered why Casper didn't believe him," she said, describing his mood.

She doesn't enter the interview unprepared. Aware that the article deals with issues she can't ignore, Navazelskis calls Casper the night before. She might be able to get answers to questions that remain open to him. But, she explains to me, an oral history interview is not an interrogation. And doesn't want to resemble it in the slightest way. It's all about the experience and perception of the interviewee. How does he remember his life; what does he recall as a direct witness to what happened. Navazelskis is interested in what it was like to be "a participant" in historical events.

The oral history project consists of countless personal histories. As an interviewer, Navazelskis can help bring chronology into focus. She provides context when it is necessary to situate personal events in relation to the landmarks in the wider history of countries and communities. But there is no intention to contradict the interviewees' memories. She has, she confesses, had to put aside the self-evident mistrust of the journalist she once was. Judging is not part of her assignment. She collects micro histories with respect for each person. In that sense, she unconditionally stands by Mekas during the interview.

It is an instructive experience to see Mekas speak for six hours in one continuous recording. I can look at him and listen as if he's sitting across from me. Navazelskis's empathy gives him every opportunity to tell his story, from his earliest childhood memories to the years in which life in Biržai and the surrounding area lost its normal routine.

It is striking that before the world fire reached Lithuania, his youth was mainly colored by the desire to go to school. His father and mother demanded that he worked on the farm. In the harvest months, there was no time for school. Simply mapping out the chronology of his repeatedly broken school years racks Navazelskis's brain. What becomes visible is an inquisitive young boy with great expectations.

Even when Mekas was shepherding, he was carrying a book with him. The young Jonas plundered the local library and yearned for a life as a poet. Despite all the nostalgia in his poetry for the simple peasant life, he seemed destined to get away from it. The diligent existence of his parents was a beautiful metaphor for a life in harmony with nature, but it certainly was no dream of a future for himself. Who would he have become, you wonder, if the war hadn't driven him to New York?

The interview also shows memory at work. A faltering memory then, in which only a few events survived as vivid anecdotes. Everything that happened in between has disappeared. The efforts to give a picture of this seem to be mainly an attempt to meet the interviewer's wishes. A crystal-clear memory is rarely found.

Mekas is easily disturbed by questions that remind him that he has forgotten a lot. The longer I watch, the more his stutter appears to me as a sign of helplessness. Not of Mekas as a person, but of his memory. As if his memory doesn't belong to him, but to an outsider, with whom he has to beg not to abandon him.

Mekas indicates more than once that he has to rely on "deduction," something Navazelskis obviously does not want: she wants unmediated experiences. The facts that Casper presented to Mekas (in the form of photocopies and history books) and to which Navazelskis sometimes subtly steers, have visibly made him doubt the reliability of his memory. Which is something else than doubting the memories that (although with difficulty) do appear to his mind's eye. What can he do other than to trust them? In his own way.

In the meticulous transcription that the Holocaust Museum makes of all interviews, this is how it reads:

> "Sure, when I'm talking about, you know now, around the questions here, and I'm sort of trying to get to it. You see, intuitively, and as a poet, and who sort of was there, and some of it I remember like un-directly, and un-directly, I know that I'm right, but I cannot feel — put my — you know, fingers on — on — on — on — on facts, on specifics, that I'm no — I know that I'm right un-direct, about the feelings of the people there. I know — remember very clearly, you know, sort of, you know, what I heard — some glimpses out there, and I don't need everything literally, from A to Z to make my — my — my observations, yes."

Mekas struggles for six hours through the "fleeting impressions" that his memory still offers him. Save when he can fall back on one of his frequently repeated anecdotes, then some amusement glows behind his eyes, the addiction of the popular conversationalist. If something becomes clear, then this: Mekas has handed in the novel of his life and would prefer not to change a word. He's finished writing. Too bad Casper is trying to be the stern and demanding editor of it.

Why would anyone need an editor if the story were already good? Take the anecdote about the first photo

Mekas took, a story that in light of his later film career easily could acquire the luster of a myth.

In the spring of 1940, his older brother Povilas gave Mekas a photo camera as a present. He patiently waits for a good moment to take his first photograph. He only has one film, so he has to be frugal. Then Russian tanks roll into Lithuania. Growling columns in impressive clouds of dust pass by his parental farm. The young Jonas runs out of the house, leaving his parents terrified behind. From a rock he takes one picture after the other. The euphoria is short-lived, as a Russian officer dashes towards him. He grabs the camera, pulls the film out of it, and tramples it under his boots. He shouts to him in Russian to run away. Jonas doesn't need a second word for that, and rushes back home. His first contribution to the photographic arts, he will be only too happy to tell, is trampled under the boots of a Russian soldier.

In a version on a Facebook page, Mekas experiences the same story as a sixteen-year-old. He is sixteen after December 22, 1938, i.e. most of 1939. The Red Army invades Lithuania on June 15, 1940. Mekas knows that too, so he situates the incident in the summer of 1940. Then he is seventeen, and half a year on his way to eighteen, one learns by simple arithmetic. Figures and data are not Mekas's strongest point, but why do I care?

The anecdote is a Mekas myth in optima forma. Fate has predestined young Jonas to follow the path of the arts. A path that he must tread unbiased and in utter innocence. The naivety of his very first use of his camera has surprised his Russian attacker so much that it has saved his life. With a camera you can exorcise evil.

But when I watch the oral history interview, I hope to get a glimpse beyond the myth. Issues have piled up that I finally want to sort out. My research has lost its permissiveness.

Three questions return in my notes: Has Mekas realized that his work with the two magazines could be understood as collaboration? What did Mekas know about the mass murder of the Jews in Biržai? Why did he flee to Germany in 1944, at the same time as the German troops are retreating from the Baltic States? These questions are explosive because with every one of them Casper puts forward information that compromises Mekas. That is, if you take the moral subtext of them into account and you consider them in the light of collaboration.

What does Mekas have to contribute to this in the interview? In any case, no facts. He has little to contradict the truth of hard data and documents. What Mekas can offer is *context* (besieged by two totalitarian powers shortly after each other in a country that finally thought itself to be independent), *personal circumstances* (Biržai is in a remote corner of Lithuania, far away from the news; his character didn't allow him to observe things that were too horrible) and his *own version* of events (how a partisan urged him to leave Biržai as soon as possible).

Context, circumstances, version — all three the swampy domain of interpretation. It forces me to weigh, consider, judge, adjust. It comes down to asking the stuttering Mekas to take up his own defense, which any lawyer or judge would discourage a suspect to do. First of all, of course, the question is whether one can expect of seventy-year-old events, which were not cast in the concrete of the successful anecdote, the accurate representation that I am now demanding. To what extent can you build a case on Mekas's memories at all?

It is not difficult to find an expert witness who puts the reliability of memories into perspective. For a novel, I once studied the work of Willem Wagenaar, the forensic psychologist who became internationally known as an expert witness in the trial of John Demjanjuk, who after a long and confusing trial turned out not to be Treblinka's "Iwan the Terrible," but a perhaps no less terrible guard in the Sobibor extermination camp. Anyone who wants to prove the unreliability of memories, especially the use of unreliable witness statements in court cases, will find an abundance of examples in Wagenaar's research.

According to Wagenaar, a trial is a competition between stories. Which story does the judge (and in Anglo-Saxon countries, the jury) think is best corroborated by the facts? Which story is most synchronous with the available evidence? Even if someone confesses, Wagenaar emphasizes, that story should be anchored in irrefutable and factual evidence. If not, a confession is meaningless. People can remember events that never took place. Memories will move with the stories others add to them. Every interrogator is therefore a potential polluter of the confession. There is no need for malicious intent behind this — it is rather incompetence, Wagenaar likes to point out.

The pure memory, the memory that coincides exactly with whatever has happened, does not exist. Events become a story immediately after they have taken place, or more precisely: several stories from the various people involved. And not everyone is an equally good observer or storyteller. Judicial errors are almost always based on an excessive reliance on witness statements or confessions. A reliance that goes back to nothing more than an unconditional — and incomprehensible, Wagenaar states — belief in the possibility of pure remembrance.

(I have an amusing personal memory of Willem Wagenaar in the light of this essay. Wagenaar collected nineteenth-century magic lanterns and slides. In his spare time, he used them to perform enchanting shows. When I worked at the Netherlands Filmmuseum in the nineties, he regularly used to perform there during Christmas time. With the forerunner of the film projector he brought the ingenious, mechanical slides to life. Phantasmagorias, Victorian melodramas, kaleidoscopic images, starry skies and visual jokes — Wagenaar enjoyed bringing the imagination to life as an *explicateur*, making up stories completely free from the demands he made in his daily work of finding legal truth.)

However, it does not help to put aside every testimony on the basis of a desperate relativism. In his introduction to *Remembering Survival: Inside a Nazi Slave-Labor Camp*, historian Christopher Browning recalls the trial that had put him on the trail of the Starachowiche labor camp, the subject of his study. In a 1972 criminal trial of Walther Becker, head of the German security police in the Polish industrial city of Starachowiche between 1941 and 1945, several Jewish survivors made incriminating statements about his brutal actions during the deportations in the region. Starachowiche was not an extermination camp, so there were relatively many survivors who could testify against Becker. Becker denied everything.

To the dismay of everyone who followed the case, the German judge on duty acquitted Becker. His justification: witness statements are the most unreliable kind of evidence. He then reviewed each statement to identify inconsistencies and contradictions with other statements in the smallest details. In the eyes of the judge, no testimony could be trusted one hundred percent. He demanded a perfection of the survivors' memories, according to Browning, "nowhere to be found in the real world."

In contrast to that judge, Browning was not prepared to let Becker get away with it so easily. If the German legal system allowed Becker to escape, he figured, "I felt that at least he could be given his appropriate place in historian's hell."

Browning is a historian who does not, like many of his colleagues, shy away from using individual testimonies as a primary source. Based on official interrogations with members of the Reserve Unit 101 of the German *Ordnungspolizei* (Order Police) about their role in the Holocaust, he wrote *Ordinary Men*, a crushing reconstruction of the daily practice of massacring entire Jewish communities in rural Poland. In spite of the fact that the interrogations took place some twenty years after the events and each of the interviewees tried to evade legal persecution, as a result of which lying often seemed wiser than the honest truth, it turned out to be possible to gain insight into the mass murders which had occurred outside the extermination camps on the basis of the stories of the perpetrators.

In his meticulous reconstructions, Browning revealed how with careful contextualization, weighing and differentiation, oral memories are as valuable to historiography as written documents and dry statistics. His reconstructions are so convincing precisely because he has an eye for inconsistencies, the anomalous detail and for individuals (whether perpetrator or victim) who do not conform to the usual image of the behavior of the group to which they belong. By daring to change perspective, he arrives at insights that bypass the reduction of the black-and-white scheme.

His research into the behavior of Reserve Unit 101 in occupied Poland shows that there is no unequivocal explanation why "ordinary men" indulge in rabid killings. Latent anti-Semitism, years of Nazi propaganda, simple opportunism, the inability to resist group pressure and the importance of camaraderie form an opaque amalgam within which each individual has made his own considerations. Browning came to discover that it was possible for German men to evade the task of participating in the mass murders without punishment. This makes the participation of the majority of the ordinary men of Reserve Unit 101 even more puzzling, not least of those who had remained far removed from Nazi ideology in the 1930s. It proved to be possible to make individual choices, is Browning's message.

That is why every individual deserves to be heard, without making a judgment in advance. In Browning's *Ordinary Men* one is often reading with bated breath the atrocities that individuals are capable of, but it is downright unbearable that by presenting the murderers as individuals he presents you with a question that can hardly be answered: Would you have succeeded in not being a follower?

Then for his later book, *Remembering Survival*, in which Browning reconstructs everyday life in a Nazi slave labor camp, he mainly made use of testimonials from survivors.* They had no reason to hide behind fabricated statements. Also in this case, many decades after the events, he could not count on the consistency that the German judge would have demanded, but he learned that if you put all those testimonies together and weigh them against each other, you do have "a core memory" that "has remained basically stable despite the passage of time."

It in no way blinded him to the fundamentally problematic relationship between event and memory. Browning recognized four ways in which his eyewitnesses dealt with memories. Events could have been suppressed, simply because the memory is incapable of making room for them. In that case, the event no longer exists, and the "witness" is unable to revive it, even though others may claim to have been there. There are also memories that are secret. The event is known to the witness, but too painful to share. Most of the time these are memories that have to do with a feeling of guilt. Stealing a loaf of bread from a fellow prisoner, for example, is unbearable to admit publicly. There are also memories (and therefore events) that can only be shared with other victims. Outside the group, the idea is, they will not be understood.

* It can hardly be surprising that Ina Navazelskis drew my attention to Browning's introduction to *Remembering Survival*.

And then there are the public memories, by far the most, which are shared, but to which another danger clings. They are often contaminated by "iconic Holocaust tropes," stylistic figures from the popular imaginary of deportations, camps and massacres in novels, films and history books. Survivors try to synchronize their memories with testimonials such as those of Primo Levi, Browning noted, whereas his experiences in Auschwitz are not comparable to much lesser-known massacres such as those in Lithuania in 1941, where the likelihood of survival was much less and, no matter how brutal this may sound, therefore left far fewer eyewitness accounts.

The four categories of Browning can easily be projected on the role that memory plays in every human life. Each of us has our gaps, secrets, shared confidences and loudly articulated memories. It is the circumstances of war and mass murder that give memories or their absence such a hard-to-bear weight. After all, the moral judgment of history must be done right. The veracity of the truth is at stake. Holocaust and genocide historians in particular feel that weight. In the face of such a massive and unspeakable injustice, it is impossible to accept the daily failings of memory as an excuse.

I suspect that this is why Casper attacks Mekas so hard, even though there are no demonstrable crimes linked to Mekas, as the facts make no mention of individual atrocities, nor of inflammatory anti-Semitism.

Casper does not address Mekas for his deeds, but for his memories: the forgotten mass murder of 2,400 Jews.

This is something I have to remind myself over and over again: in "the Mekas case" *memory is on trial* – that's the uniqueness of it, but also a fact that can easily be overseen.

Of course, putting Mekas's memory on trial does not reduce the importance of what he did or did not do. To reach a verdict, Casper has to compare the dry documents from the archives with the less dry testimonies of Mekas. He investigates the distance between fact and memory. How far apart they are permitted to be. To do this, Casper must investigate what "happened." The six-hour oral history interview by the USHMM, appearing chronologically in response to the article, can thus be interpreted as an interrogation, even though it was conducted by the empathic Navazelskis and not by the dogged Casper.

An interrogation also means that Mekas is given the opportunity to tell his story in his own words. That sounds simpler than it is. The spoken word is difficult to translate into a written testimonial. In the transcription made by the Holocaust Museum, Mekas can hardly be followed. On paper, he is a scatterbrain; in the video recording, a man who has difficulty finding his words. To make his testimony readable, I will have to summarize and edit Mekas. Every published interview makes use of this, but when it comes to precision, can you still refer to it as "Mekas in his own words"? When does grammar take over and the factuality of the spoken word disappear into a well-formed sentence or narrative? When will it become a story I tell? And with what right? Wagenaar emphasizes that even a report of the offense follows imperceptibly the dramaturgical laws of a novel or film. Every written story adapts to a structure in which a beginning, middle and an end is a compelling stylistic figure, otherwise it becomes incomprehensible. But does it do justice to the disorder that characterizes our lives?

Another complication that hardly seems solvable to me is whether I can measure up to Casper when it comes to weighing Mekas's claims. As a historian, Casper has a massive lead. He presumably speaks (or at least, reads) Lithuanian and Hebrew, wrote his dissertation on Lithuania during the interwar period, has the political and military events on hand, has himself browsed the newspaper layers in the archives and was able to ask a renowned Lithuanian colleague for advice. Moreover, he is much better acquainted with recent literature and generally accepted views on the Holocaust in Lithuania, which were dramatically revised after independence in 1991.

As I leaf through my pile of collected articles on the history of Lithuania, I notice that I have to be alert to that shift. It has become clear to me that there is a new version of that history, in which the role of Lithuanian civilian militias and civil servants in the mass murder of the Jews is no longer denied or concealed. Also, historians have their paradigms. The current paradigm is reflected in an International Commission for the Evaluation of the Crimes of the Nazi and Soviet Occupation Regimes in Lithuania, set up by the Lithuanian government in 1998. Participating historians have charted events almost from day to day, making use of the archives that were closed during the Soviet era. The reports can be read on the Internet (which I did) and are summarized in conclusions that sound like bureaucratic guidelines.

"Approved-Conclusions_Persecution-and-Mass-Murder-of-Lithuanian-Jews" is the title of one of the PDFs I downloaded. In it, I read chilling sentences like this one: "Indigenous cooperation considerably facilitated the persecution, ghettoization and mass murder of the Jews." Or: "The justification for these killings was the anti-Semitic propaganda equating Jews and Bolshevism." And: "Only approximately 9,000 Lithuanian Jews survived the war."

The committee distinguishes three phases in the mass murder. In the first week of the war, Lithuanian militias indulge in anti-Jewish violence, often just after the German authorities have arrived, but not under their control. Soon after, in the month of July with the help of Lithuanian support troops, ghettos are set up from which regularly Jewish men are deported and murdered. The mass extermination of the Jewish communities escalated starting in the beginning of August. The Jews were no longer accused of being Bolsheviks (which was the first motivation for the violence), but Jews. Coordinated action was initiated by a special German army task force and was assisted by Lithuanian support troops, including civil servants, policemen and volunteers from the so-called self-defense battalions set up immediately after the invasion. The *Einsatzkommando* (killing squad) in command consisted of no more than 139 German men. Each of the more than 200,000 victims was murdered by a shot in the neck. Without extensive help from Lithuanian support troops, the massacres could not have been carried out.

The Provisional Government and the Lithuanian Activist Front (LAF) spread anti-Semitic propaganda that leaves no room for misunderstanding how they envisioned the sanctity of Jewish belonging in Lithuania — a stable social pact, according to Casper's thesis, that had existed since medieval times. One paragraph in the Committee's report comes closest to what is being considered here in my writings: "While it is difficult to quantify, the attitude and mind-set of the population at large towards the murder of the Jews was an important factor in the progress of the genocide. The Commission encourages further research into the contemporary attitudes and stance of the population towards the Holocaust."

Casper can only have read this as an encouragement toward his research. The doors of the archives are open. There are still so many issues waiting to be proven, refuted, or brought to light. It explains, I suspect, his self-assurance; he has a firm paradigm on his side.

It gives Casper a head start not only on me, but also on Mekas. I cannot escape the impression that Mekas had allowed himself little knowledge of the recent paradigm shift. The question of how the mass murder of the Jews could have taken place in such a short period of time was preferably not to be discussed in post-war Lithuania. If there was any writing about it, it was mostly by Lithuanian historians who had gone into exile, including fervent nationalists who were happy to shift all the blame to Nazi Germany. Many of them, like Mekas, lived in the United States.

The facts of the current paradigm may be clear to me now, and appear to be the basis of solid evidence, but that does not mean that they are agreed upon or accepted by everyone. The history of the Jews in Lithuania has already been told and adjusted in many ways. There is not only a historiography of the facts, but also a historiography of how those facts are interpreted or represented.

Immediately after the war, the communist authorities placed a small memorial plaque in the forest of Astravas, with this text in Russian and Lithuanian: “Here are buried 3,000 Soviet citizens who were shot in 1941 by Hitler’s Fascists.” If Mekas would have had the courage to go to the forest in 1972, he could have read that. In the early nineties of the last century, after Lithuania had separated from the Soviet Union, the text was replaced. In Yiddish and Lithuanian it now reads: "At this place, Hitler's executioners and their helpers murdered about 2,400 Jews — men, women and children — on August 8, 1941, and about 90 Lithuanians." In June 2019, another monument was unveiled, with the names of 522 of the 2,400 victims that could be traced. To truly commemorate them, the prevailing notion now is, we need names, as proof that they are individuals, each with their own life synthesized in the name they were given at birth.

Although in March 1995, during a state visit to Israel, President Algirdas Brazauskas formally expressed guilt about the participation of Lithuanian citizens in the Holocaust, the coming to terms with the past in Lithuania is still a difficult topic to address. It didn't take a lot of research to see that. In the eyes of many Lithuanians, coming to terms with the Soviet past deserves priority. An attitude I recognize with Mekas when he eagerly puts forward the crimes of the Soviet Union to indicate what Lithuanians suffered most. Communism and the whims of Stalin's terror directly affected the peasantry to which he belonged. His family was in immediate danger. The Nazis, on the other hand, were so busy murdering Jews and keeping the invasion of Russia going that they left Mekas and his family in peace. That sounds cynical, but war and occupation are simply reducing our loyalties to the smallest possible group to which we relate: family and relatives. It takes an uncommon courage to deviate from that perspective.

In order to muffle this uncomfortable discussion, the Lithuanian government opted for a scientific remembrance, by setting up a commission that would investigate the crimes of both the Nazis and the Soviet regime. Yet, (international) historians may describe and preserve the memory of the Holocaust in Lithuania carefully in generally accessible documents, everyone is still free to accept them, use them for self-examination, or simply dismiss them as a manipulated past.

In 2011, a monument commemorating the 72,000(!) Jews murdered in the forest of Ponary near Vilnius was daubed with a swastika and the slogan "Hitler was right." According to historian Timothy Snyder, who raised the issue on the *New York Review of Books* website, another monument not far from there made a vulgar insult to the compensation paid by the Lithuanian government to the families of murdered Jews.

At the end of 2019, Lithuanian MP and historian Arūnas Gumuliauskas proposed a law stating that "the Lithuanian state and nation did not participate in the Holocaust because they were occupied during that period." His supporters regard President Algirdas Brazauskas's apology in 1995 as a historic mistake. Lithuania is not to blame for the extermination of the Judeo-Lithuanian community, they claim. Gumuliauskas brings the processing of the war past back to where it started, in that of the denial.

"We are not responsible for the past, but we are responsible for what we choose to remember and what we choose to forget," historian Kim Wagner wrote in a letter to *The London Review of Books*. I jotted it down at the top of my research notes. The past is not just a slate that easily can be wiped clean. What matters is how we decide to read and interpret it, which often means partly wiping it out and rewriting it. If something is in control of the past, then not the past, but the present. This struggle is not only manifest in Lithuania.

Like his Lithuanian counterpart, French President Jacques Chirac did not make an official apology to the deported Jews until 1995. The only difference is that the closed archives of the Soviets could not be used as an excuse for this late admission of guilt. The Vichy regime, which ruled France between 1940 and 1944, actively cooperated in the deportation of at least 76,000 Jews, of whom only 3,000 returned alive; 12,500 died outside the camps. On the other hand, of the 340,000 registered Jews in France, 75% survived the war, one of the highest survival rates of all occupied countries.

Of the 140,000 Jews registered in the Netherlands

(my country) in May 1940, 101,800 did not survive the deportations. Of the Western European countries, the Netherlands has the highest percentage of Jewish victims, which most historians attribute to the willingness of government agencies (civil servants, police, railway personnel) to cooperate with the registrations and deportations. Eichmann spoke with admiration about Dutch efficiency. Although it was (mostly) not Dutch persons who pulled the trigger, the percentage of 73% Dutch victims is close to the 95% of Lithuania. Nevertheless, successive Dutch governments waited until 2020 with a public apology to the victims and survivors of the deportations (Jews, Sinti, Roma and homosexuals).

In Casper's view, Mekas has shied away from the responsibility of choosing between what he thinks he ought to remember and what he does not. It can't hurt to point out that he wasn't the only one with a gap in his memory. That's not an excuse, but a conclusion.

Which brings me to the next complication: where do I myself stand in relation to all this?

The way in which Mekas describes his life under war and occupation forces me to examine my own moral values. I don't know on which side of the line my tractable character would take me during an occupation by a foreign power. Sure, I dream of courage and steadfastness, but are these given to me when it comes down to it? Still, my own uncertainty about this doesn't stop me from expressing my research on Mekas in judicial phrasing, I notice. It slips into my language, simply because there seems to be no pure or neutral language for it.

The three questions in my notes are easy to adjust. Not: Are you allowed to work for a magazine that has been co-opted? But: Is working for such a magazine under an occupying power an understandable choice? Not: Can you overlook a mass murder of 2,400 Jewish citizens? But: Can a mass murder be too gruesome to allow it into your emotional household? Not: Are you allowed to forget something like that? But: Is it possible to forget such a thing? Not: Has Mekas fled the Red Army? But: If you have to choose between two evils, is a flight to Nazi Germany permissible?

How far apart are these "not" and "but" questions actually? Don't they sound like the dilemmas with which every human life has been veined? I encounter them every day, in minor, harmless situations. No matter how innocent, can I vouch for the fact that my actions (or not acting, or forgetting) have never harmed the happiness of others? For someone who has to endure in circumstances of war and occupation, these types of questions suddenly take on a painful urgency. Those who are strict and convinced of their own righteousness can be tempted to give easy answers. Those who are less strict, or do not trust their own righteousness in advance, will probably find the answers a little less obvious.

Even so, between those two positions it is easy to commute. That's how it turns out every time I think about Mekas. My position changes just as easily from irreconcilable to condoning and back. Perhaps this is inevitable with every human life that is brought before us for judgment. Consistency and coherence can streamline stories, anecdotes and Mekas-myths as beautifully as ever, but Peter at the Gate of Heaven, how should that poor wretch fare in his daily work?

No single history can be summarized satisfactorily when it comes to an individual's role in it, and certainly not in the point-by-point, scholastic enumerations used by Lithuania's international "truth commission." It relieves the individual of his or her responsibilities. It reduces victims, perpetrators and bystanders to puppets of which a blind fate has been in control. Transparency can thus mutate into a harmless form of closure. Read the approved conclusions, and we will proceed to business as usual.

Personal testimonies give history back to those who affected it, no matter how confusing and inconsistent their accounts may be. Therein lies the importance of Mekas's own story. That does not alter the fact that he is regularly the victim of my frustration. Irritations, I am increasingly aware of, which do not so much apply to Mekas (although I'm sure that's how it sounds), but above all to the situations to which the tremors of history have condemned someone like Mekas. I can imagine the powerlessness that comes over you when every act, committed in complete ignorance of the future, is weighed afterwards as if that future had been clearly in your sight. We live in the immediacy of the moment, history judges from an inexorable later.

Now that I want to move on to the next chapters, about to relate to the speaking Mekas, I suddenly realize that I am no longer in conversation with the artist Jonas Mekas. From now on he is a random Lithuanian citizen whom I call to account for his actions between 1939 and 1945. How much does Mekas differ from all those millions who have never been questioned or interrogated? He is one of many, of whose testimonials accidentally have been handed down, of whose facts can be found and diaries have been kept (however, those from before July 19, 1944, unfortunately not).

I notice, to my dismay and annoyance, that I constantly have to remind myself that Mekas is not a criminal. If the whole story had taken place in the Netherlands, the Press Purification Committee after the war would have banned the two periodicals for which Mekas wrote. He himself would have been left alone after a brief interrogation. Which does not detract from the fact that it would undoubtedly have been thrown in his way at some later stage. If Mekas had stayed in Lithuania, the Stalinist authorities would almost certainly have judged him differently. His work for the magazines the Germans tolerated and his anti-Stalin poem were enough to deport him to the Gulag for five or ten years, which, in Western eyes, would have absolved him of any guilt. In the United States, far from the closed Soviet archives, no one came up with the idea of investigating Mekas's movements. First covered by the Cold War (the Soviets were the bad guys), then by his left-wing activism in the sixties (protesting the Vietnam war; challenging censorship, supporting gay rights), and finally by his canonization as an advocate of avant-garde cinema (the acclaimed founder of Anthology Archives, hero of the festivals).

Casper has added a new and unexpected scenario. Mekas's memory versus objective history, the value of personal memories versus the firmness of facts — that is the battleground in which I now venture to find my way.

m a g a z i n e

Mekas never made a secret of his working for two weekly newspapers between 1941 and 1944, although he never mentioned them by name. Casper went looking for them. In Biržai, Mekas worked for *Naujosios Biržų žinios* (*The New Biržai News*, or *NBZ*). After completing high school, he worked from 1943 in the larger town of Panevėžys for *Panevėžio Apygardos Balsas* (*The Panevėžys Region Voice*, or

PAB). Although Mekas in the introduction of *I Had Nowhere to Go* calls himself “editor-in-chief” and “technical editor” and he tells Casper that he was “more or less in charge” of both publications, he later takes that back as bragging. To Navazelskis he explains that he owed the jobs to his perfect spelling, which means that he now situates his position closer to “technical-editor” than to “editor-in-chief.”

According to Casper, the *NBZ* in Biržai was one of five regional magazines established by the Lithuanian Activist Front immediately after the invasion of the Germans. Mekas calls the newspaper and thus indirectly the LAF “patriotic.” Most historians (at least those after 1991) have been less positive about the LAF. Following the Soviet occupation in 1940, their leaders retreated to Berlin under the protection of the Nazis. Fanatically anti-communist and extremely nationalistic, the LAF supported the German invasion of the Soviet Union. Just before the German offensive (known as Operation Barbarossa), the LAF proclaimed Lithuanian independence and appointed a provisional pro-German government. Lithuanian soldiers were called upon to rise up against the Soviet occupier. One of the first actions of the government was to pass laws that deprived Jews of their citizenship and forced them to wear the yellow Star of David. The Lithuanian Jews were outlawed overnight.

In this lawless vacuum, sections of the LAF and so-called self-defense groups committed the first anti-Semitic excesses, although there was no such thing as massive pogroms. This was an important nuance in the paradigm of the committee of inquiry because, according to the investigators, the direction of German *Einsatzgruppen* (Special Task Forces) was crucial to the massacres. There were relatively many secular Jews among the communist bureaucrats during the first Soviet occupation, who had previously been excluded from administrative functions in the highly segregated Lithuania. No matter how few there were in absolute terms, they were visible for the first time as public administrators. It turned out to be a convenient way of linking latent anti-Semitism among the population to hatred against the Soviets, who, after previous deportations, had randomly deported 20,000 citizens (intellectuals, shopkeepers, artisans, farmers) to the Siberian Gulag just before the German invasion. Among them were relatively many Jews, who thus saw their chances of surviving the war increase indefinitely — the course of history often explores the extremes of cynicism. In the propaganda of the LAF, however, communism was presented, wholly in sync with Hitler's idea-fixe, as part of the "Jewish conspiracy": that Jews and Bolsheviks conspired to dominate the world. The majority of Jewish Lithuanians had no idea that this could concern them at all.

According to Casper, it is precisely this propaganda for which the *NBZ* lent itself, even after the

German occupying forces soon sidelined the LAF and the provisional government because of their nationalist agenda. Nevertheless, the magazine continued to publish pro-German and anti-Semitic propaganda. Casper: "One of Mekas's poems, 'For a Young Friend,' is printed in a grid of poems that includes Matuzevičius's 'To the Honorable German Soldier'; another tribute by Matuzevičius was titled 'We're with the Führer.' A front-page editorial from the first issue declared, 'We are humans, not Bolshevist Jewish materialist ape-people.'"

On the Vilnius-based website Defending History, which advocates keeping the memory of the Holocaust alive, reference is made to an editorial on the front page of July 26, 1941, with the ominous title (translated) "Guidelines for National Work" that ends like this: "The Lithuanian nation must be cleansed of minorities. The minority question in Lithuania was relevant before June 15, 1940,* as well, but at the time was not properly dealt with. Today this matter has taken on a new phase. The question of minorities has been decided and all that is left is to properly deal with it." Two weeks later it became clear how definitively the LAF had imagined dealing with the Jewish "minority."

Mekas's transition from *NBZ* to *PAB* in Panevėžys,

* Following the Molotov-Ribbentrop Pact, Lithuania was occupied by Soviet troops on this day. Shortly afterwards Lithuania became a constituent republic of the Soviet Union.

some sixty kilometers south of Biržai, was a promotion. According to him, the *PAB* was a literary magazine with a few pages devoted to news. Casper: "The European Holocaust Research Infrastructure, an EU-funded archival resource based in Holland, uses three subject tags to describe the paper: 'Nazi policies,' 'Propaganda' and 'Antisemitic propaganda.'" What Casper reads confirms that signature. He finds articles praising the German victories on the Eastern Front and articles with titles such as "The Jewish War." An essay by Mekas on the Lithuanian writer and political activist Vincas Kudirka is next to a villainous piece about three Jews who are said to have disguised themselves as Lithuanians.

Towards the end of 1944, both *NBZ* and *PAB* call on Lithuanians to register as workers in German factories, in order to support the fight against Bolshevism.

In their dry form, these are facts that sound painful. Mekas tells Casper that he does not remember the pro-German propaganda and anti-Semitic articles. He cannot dispute Casper's photocopies. To Navazelskis, Mekas explains that the front pages may have been reserved for pro-German proclamations, but that the other pages were outside the control of the Nazis. They published about the history of Lithuania and folk art.

Navazelskis endeavors to take a different approach. When she looks at newspapers like this, she explains to Mekas, she has the feeling that the sections that are not propaganda do legitimize the propaganda. Is he aware of that hazard?

"We didn't see it that way," Mekas replies. It was a matter of give and take towards the occupier, he explains. The propaganda wasn't theirs, but the Germans. He and the readership were only interested in the other articles. It was a way of outsmarting the Germans. Sure, you can close all the theaters and shut down the entire cultural infrastructure, but that's not what life under occupation looks like: "People continue to try to live, not to be disturbed by it, and try to continue their lives normally, and ignore, and sort of like to fight indirectly, in [...] very invisible ways, the occupation."

It is easy, says Mekas, to judge this now in a free America, seventy-five years later: "You are not there. You are from the outside, a different context." It was only through Casper that he realized what the LAF stood for and recognized their malignant role in the provisional government.

Had he never heard of the Lithuanian Activist Front, Navazelskis asks as neutrally as possible. "Not then," Mekas answers confidently. He first heard about it "by the guy who wrote the article." In Semeniškiai he also had no knowledge of their revolt against the Soviets just before the Germans invaded Lithuania. Nor about their role in the mass murder of the Jews. Semeniškiai was simply too far away from all the news.

How ill informed or naive can a well-read poet be? Casper is clear about it in his email: "[Navazelskis's] videotaped interview does show to some extent how, like in my interviews, Mekas avoided addressing questions and fell back on telling familiar stories. It is unfortunate that, in the USHMM interview, Mekas says many of the same implausible things as he did with me — for example claiming to have never heard of the Lithuanian Activist Front until I told him — with no direct challenge. Because the museum lent an imprimatur to his stories, some writers in the media made it seem like Mekas had cleared the air in the interview, or even told the whole truth for the first time, which is not the case."

These were times in which everything that makes life meaningful was put on edge, so much is for sure. In order to get a grip on Mekas, I searched for parallel stories, for other lives in similar circumstances. While the history books may be clear (about dates, publications, verified events), Mekas takes the view that for individual lives that clarity does not apply. Historiography (if not every form of written record) doesn't know what to do with the incongruities of life. It may not be methodologically sound, but I feel that it helps me to compare Mekas's life with that of others. If the past is made up of countless micro histories, and if the individual is at the heart of the smallest possible history, then the experiences of others can help to understand an individual's choices and actions.

Such as the micro-history of Algirdas Greimas. He is only five years older than Mekas and is living in Šiauliai when the German troops march in, about a hundred kilometers west of Biržai. His parents belong to the middle class: his father, a teacher and education inspector; his mother, a secretary. The first years of Greimas's life are spent in the countryside, but unlike Mekas the summer months on the farms in his village are Arcadian excursions; he doesn't lose valuable teaching years with them. From the age of ten, the family settles in Šiauliai, an industrial town, and the fourth largest city in Lithuania. Four years later the family moves to Marijampolė, another industrial town of a certain size. Greimas completes his secondary schooling there.

Mekas and Greimas share a passion for literature. But where Mekas has only the local library, Greimas is surrounded by kindred spirits with whom he can share his intellectual discoveries. The disputes of the inter-war period do not pass the young Greimas unnoticed. Years later, in what he calls an attempt to write his intellectual autobiography, he remembers the fervor that captivated his friends and contemporaries: "It was as if they were responding to an unholy need to take action, which haunted everyone and urged them to action by any means, to do something, no matter what, to break something at any price [...]. A young person would become a Fascist or a Communist solely due to their environment or circumstances." Similarly, Mekas remembered that from his bedroom he overheard his older brothers and their friends discussing political issues with voices raised. He himself is still too young to take part in them.

Greimas's student years are much more privileged than those of the farmer's son Mekas. At the end of the thirties, he gets the chance to study in France. The Lithuanian government of dictator Antanas Smetona was seeking an educational model that would shirk the influence of the nations the small country felt itself threatened by: Germany, Poland, the Soviet Union. The independent Lithuania hopes to find a shining model in France, a nationalistic ideal that sends many students with scholarships to French universities. In 1939, Greimas is called back and conscripted. After a confusing period, during which he had to serve under the banner of the Red Army, he returned to Šiauliai in 1940 and started working as a teacher at a girls' high school.

Compared to Mekas, the young Greimas is a world citizen. He has traveled beyond the borders of Lithuania. Mekas had to rely on literature for this. For both men, the war is a no man's land in which they have to search and grope their way. Both make careers after the war, Mekas in New York, Greimas in Paris, where he becomes a famous linguist and together with Roland Barthes one of the leading figures in semiotics.

Greimas dies in 1992, aged seventy-four. Unlike Mekas, he has always remained polemic and politically involved in what was going on in Lithuania. He wrote in Lithuanian magazines published outside his native country and never lost hope that Lithuania would once again become a "European" state. He only just experienced the secession from the Soviet Union, not the accession to the European Union. And he didn't have to experience a dispute about his "war past" himself.

In 2017, the 13th World Congress of Semiotics in Kaunas, which took place in honor of Greimas in Lithuania, was taken aback by a pamphlet asking for one minute's silence for "the victims of Greimas." Andrius Kulikauskas, lecturer in philosophy and ethics at the Vilnius Gediminas Technical University, accused Greimas of collaborating on *Tėvynė* (*Fatherland*), a Lithuanian weekly newspaper that appeared in Šiauliai and just like *NBZ* was controlled by the Lithuanian Activist Front. Kulikauskas claimed that he could prove that Greimas was responsible for an anti-Semitic editorial on the "Jewish question," under the title (in the English translation of Kulikauskas) "Enough with the Softness Towards the Jews." The reason why the "softness towards the Jews" had to end: "The Jewish force [...] for a long time parasitically sucked the Lithuanian body, drawing its sap." The editorial in *Tėvynė* calls for a radical solution: "The order issued by the city's administration regarding the transfer of the Jews needs to be implemented and all decent Lithuanians must contribute to this work."

On June 29, 1941, this radical solution was undertaken in the Kužiai forest, twelve kilometers northwest of Šiauliai. Thousands of Jews were murdered that day. According to The Holocaust Atlas of Lithuania website, which offers an interactive map with details about murders such as these, there were up to 8,000 victims in the Kužiai forest by the end of the summer.

In order to "unmask" Greimas as author of the article, Kulikauskas in my opinion needs a lot of circumstantial evidence. In any case, his historical research looks less solid than that of Casper. However, Kulikauskas did not convince Greimas's biographers and the organizers of the congress. As with Mekas, his admirers have a tendency towards hagiography. I know several people who studied with Greimas; they never spoke about him except with great admiration. His charisma must have resembled that of Mekas.

No hidden fact has been revealed either, because just like Mekas, Greimas never made a secret of the fact that immediately after the German invasion he worked as an editor for a newspaper, in his case named *Tėvynė*. Both of them obviously saw no reason to hide anything. I suspect that also in "the Greimas case" nobody saw the need to browse through the archived *Tėvynė*. Kulikauskas was the first to stand up for the victims of the campaign against the Jewish community in the newspaper of which Greimas was editor.

Is Greimas's life during the war and occupation now definitely scarred by "guilt"? Even the angry Kulikauskas (who in his exasperation is more explicit than Casper in *NYRB*) must acknowledge that the many ambiguous positions in which the events of 1940 and 1941 could entangle a young intellectual in Lithuania have inevitably made Greimas. Communist or fascist? If only it were that simple. Greimas had to take many turns in those years; circumstances did not leave him a straight path.

Fascinated by the international solidarity of communism, he was at first openly sympathetic to Lithuania's accession to the Soviet Union, although his first serious amorous relationship, with left-wing activist Hania Lukauskaitė, may have contributed to this. A personal drama must have turned that idea upside down. It is in June, shortly before the German invasion, that without any reason his father and mother are arrested in Marijampolė and deported to the Gulag. Greimas would never see them again. Stalin revealed to Greimas his true face of terror and arbitrariness where it could affect him deepest.

It must have made him sensitive to the commitment of an independent Lithuania. When the Germans moved in, he briefly joined the "fascist" and "nationalist" Lithuanian Activist Front. But already after his first assignment by the German command to round up a hundred Jews to wipe the streets of Šiauliai clean, he withdrew from the hastily assembled militia. Greimas remembers feeling "[...] that something was not right. I conveyed the order, but the next morning, I didn't return to further 'liberate' the homeland." However, it didn't keep him from working as an editor for *Tėvynė*, in which anti-Semitic appeals are launched by the LAF, just like in Biržai's *NBZ*.

Greimas moves to Kaunas and in 1942–43 joins Lietuvos laisvės kovotojų sąjunga (The Union of Lithuanian Freedom Fighters, LLKS), a quaint mishmash of fascist LAF nationalists, fervent anti-communists and equally fervent anti-Nazis. If anything marks the confusion of those years, it is this barely imaginable alliance of partisans. Later, in an interview with *Le Monde*, he would say: "In this absurd situation, we had to organize the resistance against the Germans, right? But to what end? So that the Russians could move in? The resistance was an absurd resistance." He responds by writing an essay on the first complete Lithuanian translation of the *Don Quixote* that is published in 1942: "The noble Hidalgo comes at a time when we require his assistance and advice perhaps the most. In the terrible collision of the giants of this world, our small and dear country desperately needs just such naive belief in its human cultural mission."

Greimas himself is naive enough to edit *Laisvės kovotojas* (*The Freedom Fighter*), one of the three

And did people talk about it, Navazelskis tries, about these events? "Not much," replies Mekas. It elicits from Navazelskis a terrified "No, huh?" It was too horrible, Mekas explains, farmers then let things pass: "... the life goes on..."

That's the moment I'm shocked. "The life goes on" is one of those phrases Mekas likes to use in *As I Was Moving Ahead Occasionally I Saw Brief Glimpses of Beauty*. Not occasionally, but often, to mark the happy home-movie life: "life goes on... and on..." and the sunlight shimmers in the lace curtain of his New York loft, while from under the crumpled sheets Hollis in love is watching him, the children, funny tumblers, practicing their first steps, friends toast to whatever one can, the publication of a book, a new film, friendship.

Is it shame that has erected a wall in Mekas's memory? Shame about indifference that has disguised itself as forgetting, making him opt for a double denial now that Casper has pointed that out to him with his photocopies?

Where do these 2,400 Jews actually come from? From Biržai? With only its 5,000 inhabitants?

How shrill this contrasts with that speech in 1966: "... it all happened right before my eyes — before my eyes the heads of children were smashed with bayonets."

When in our Skype conversation I tell Ina Navazelskis that I find it difficult to believe Mekas, she advises me to watch another interview she did for the USHMM oral history project in 2010, eight years before she interviewed Mekas.

Algimantas Gureckas is about six months younger than Mekas and grew up until his puberty in Tauragė, more than two hundred kilometers southwest of Biržai, in a region that Hitler would later designate as inhabited by *Volksdeutsche*. The family moves to Panevėžys, where his father finds a job as a civil servant and Algimantas finishes high school. The town is about sixty kilometers from Biržai. Mekas was to become the "technical-editor" of *The Panevėžys Regional Voice* in 1943. Gureckas by that time has already settled in Vilnius and, like Greimas, has joined the Union of Lithuanian Freedom Fighters. To escape military service (the Eastern Front is inevitable), backed by his superiors in the underground, he volunteers for the *Reichsarbeitsdienst* in Germany. He is stationed on the island of Rügen. He returns to Vilnius sooner than expected, but as the Red Army advances, he too flees to Germany, where he is forced to work for the Luftwaffe. Like Mekas, he does not return to Lithuania after the war. In Munich, he reunites with his mother, who has also fled. His father is left behind in Lithuania. After studying in Germany, he manages to emigrate to the United States in 1954, where he makes a career with the American postal service.

Gureckas looks calm and amiable during the

underground newspapers in Lithuania during the war. As the editor of an officially tolerated literary magazine, he simultaneously tests the limits of what the Germans allow. When the Red Army advances, he decides to flee. Like Mekas, Greimas foresees a future in the Gulag if he stays. The Soviets do not see the partisans of the LLKS as allies, but as political opponents. For him, too, Germany is his escape route. He tries to reach France, where he has friends, but doesn't get any further than Alsace, where he goes in hiding. After the liberation, he settles in Paris and becomes the world-famous linguist, known for the "semiotic square." At the end of the seventies, I attended lectures on this subject in Nijmegen. Does that connect me to Greimas? I wouldn't have noticed his biography if I hadn't heard about him in university courses.

Lithuania and the war years continued to occupy Greimas. His memorable sentence, which summarizes the tragedy and misunderstandings of which he and Mekas have each been captives in their own way between 1939 and 1945, is this: "It is not easy to be a man and a Lithuanian, to stay faithful to oneself, one's nation and humanity."

Some wise words? Like Mekas, Greimas's memory shows a remarkable gap when it comes to the massacres of the Jews. He, too, claims never to have witnessed Lithuanian acts of violence against the Jews in Šiauliai. In the official findings of the Lithuanian "truth commission," you can read that in the first week of the war "sources confirm the attacks and killings of at least several hundred Jews in Šiauliai, carried out by *Einsatzkommando 2* [Special Task Force 2] and local Lithuanian partisans." In a few months time, this resulted in 8,000 victims. Was it possible to be blind to it? Could the Germans, with their Lithuanian auxiliary troops from a town of about 34,000 inhabitants, like a thief in the night take away 8,000 Jews without anyone noticing? Is it then possible that Mekas failed to notice the massacre of 2,400 Jews in Biržai?

the forest of Astravas

The forgotten massacre in Biržai, that's what Casper ultimately wants to take measure of Mekas's memory with. And attacks him the hardest. There are no extenuating circumstances for this lacuna, he believes, nor for evasive explanations. If Casper builds his case carefully at some point, then this is it.

Casper uncovers an interview from 1971 in which Mekas acknowledges to filmmaker Paul Sharits that he rarely speaks about his most traumatic war experiences. Only in a commencement speech for the Philadelphia College of Art in 1966, did he briefly refer to them. Casper locates the text and finds the sentence that will become the heart of his historical indictment.

Mekas tells the young, recently graduated art students about his youth during the Second World War: "I went through horrors more unbelievable than anything I had read in the books, and it all happened right before my eyes — before my eyes the heads of children were smashed with bayonets." As if he knows Wagenaar's lesson, Casper adds: "This same horrific image occurs in two key eyewitness accounts of the killings at Astravas, one of them recorded by a Jewish survivor in 1946, the other by a Lithuanian witness in 2015." Casper knows how to anchor the plausibility of a confession.

Why, I wonder, has Mekas been so reserved, or even evasive, about that history after this "confession"? Whereas at first I regarded Casper too strict in judging Mekas's forgetfulness, my annoyance towards Mekas increases when Navazelskis in the oral history interview tries to address the drama of the mass murder. It is as if everything concerning the events in the forest of Astravas has not found a compartment in Mekas's memory — or is in a closed compartment and has only escaped from it once in 1966. Mekas asks Navazelskis about the year and month of the massacre, again as if the 22nd of August 1941 did not want to connect to anything in his memory. He constantly talks about 2,200 victims ("I hear from Michael that there were 2,200"), no matter how often Navazelskis corrects that number to 2,400.

Mekas has doubts about the number, finds it hard

to believe. That many Jews didn't live in Biržai, he keeps bringing up. The town had 5,000 inhabitants. The only possibility is that Jews from surrounding villages also were forced to come to Biržai. It would explain why he did not notice the disappearing of so many Jews.

Would it matter? One in three, one in four, or one in five inhabitants have vanished within one day in a community that counted no more than five thousand souls?

Here, too, Navazelskis is carefully trying to provoke Mekas's memories. Did his parents possibly know about it? Did they know that there were Jews shot and buried in the forest of Astravas?

"They were aware of it, they did not know the details." What the family noticed was that his mother didn't come home with bagels on market days, they were no longer for sale, because there were no Jewish bakers anymore. Ring-shaped rolls – it is indeed the details that blanches a personal history from its color.

Does Mekas remember what happened to the Jewish philosopher he befriended as a boy? "I don't know," Mekas replies dryly.

And the forest of Astravas, did he ever go there after the massacre? No, he didn't. Impossible. Not even when he had to go into hiding nearby.

Did he know where it was? Yes, he did. It was hidden behind the trees, covered by a "horrible cloud," he was simply too scared by it.

interview with Navazelskis. Unlike Mekas, he does have most of the dates clear. He unerringly recognizes the sensitivities Navazelskis is trying to address. He maneuvers skillfully along delicate issues of ethnicity and nationalism. It does not prevent him from explaining in detail why the Lithuanians did not trust the Poles: because they had appropriated Vilnius and had expansionist plans; why the Jews were held to be the driving force behind the communist Soviet regime: because they were suddenly visibly involved in the government of Lithuania and were responsible for the deportations; why the Germans were seen as liberators: because they freed Lithuania from Stalinist terror. They are the well-known, condoning clichés when Lithuanians try to explain why they acted as they did (or did not act), most of which, as my readings of the "truth commission" have taught me, have mostly been numerically refuted by historians, unmasked as propaganda by the Nazis or the LAF, or nuanced as the behavior of individuals and not of entire (ethnic) communities.

Gureckas knows how to put his arguments into the foreground: cautiously and with a "we couldn't help but see it that way — then." You can sense the diplomat, whom he became as a member of the official delegation of Lithuania to the United Nations after the new independence of 1990. Unlike Mekas, he is very adept at embedding his personal memories in the collective history of Lithuania. With his "hindsight-knowledge," he knows how to summarize his life in a streamlined story. That is, until he comes to speak openly about the mass murders of the Jews. Then he is no longer cautious. Gureckas certainly hasn't stored these events in a locked compartment.

In the run-up to that, there is an impressive moment in the interview. As can be the case with the memories of a person's life story, it's a very small incident that visibly moves him. He remembers that the German offensive has been launched. Around Panevėžys, which is a small industrial town, there are bombings. He took to the streets with his hotheaded classmates, looking for weapons to defend themselves. Against who is not quite clear. Both the Soviets and the Germans act as enemies of Lithuania. In the city center, they meet a Jewish friend, a girl whom the seventeen-year-old Algimantas knows well and secretly admires. She stands in blind terror, pointing at the German fighter planes. She's doomed, she says. She's finished.

Gureckas and his friends try to reassure her. The Jewish communists will get what they deserve, but she has nothing to worry about. The Germans are a civilized nation, they say with full conviction, they won't hurt her. She doesn't want to believe them.

"We tried to tell her, you know, that there is no reason to be afraid, but she just listened and we saw that she – she just doesn't believe us, and she was right. She was right."

Gureckas and Navazelskis both fall silent. Tears glow behind his eyes. It's not hard to imagine that she was his first great, silent love.

Did he ever see her again after that meeting on the corner of that street, Navazelskis finally asks.

No. With his old classmates he sometimes wondered if she might not have survived the war after all: "... but there is no chance. There was no chance."

Most likely she was one of the 7,523 Jews who, according to the Holocaust Atlas of Lithuania, were taken from the Panevėžys ghetto to the forest of Pajuostė on August the 23rd, 1941, two weeks after the massacre in Biržai, to be shot by seventy Lithuanian gunmen and thirty Germans. "Before the shooting, each killer was given 200 grams of vodka," reports the Atlas. Among the victims were 1,609 children.

It is useful in the light of Mekas's forgetfulness to listen carefully to Gureckas's memories. In the immediate aftermath of the German invasion, Panevėžys was in a vacuum. While the Soviets were on retreat and the Germans had not yet arrived, some Lithuanians were seeking revenge. Communists were murdered, Jewish shops attacked. These were incidents, carried out by small, irregular factions. There were no systematic massacres. When the Germans arrived, Gureckas saw girls with flowers by the side of the road welcoming them. The relief that the communists had been chased away made the German troops liberators. At that moment Gureckas and his parents believed in an independence of Lithuania similar to Hungary or Slovakia. That evening the family made toasts to the new era.

The next day Gureckas immediately gets a first glimpse of what the Germans have in mind for the Jews: "I went to the police, I don't know why, [...] but I remember the view, which was very shocking to me. There was an old man, apparently a Jew, an old man, you know, and he was standing like in the corner, and on his forehead was written in, I would say maybe it looked like wet ashes, [...] *žydas*."

"So that means Jew," declares Navazelskis.

"Jew," confirms Gureckas. The image has always stayed with him.

After their final exams, a friend invites Gureckas to his sister's wedding. He lives in a village not far from Biržai. The friend shows him the small town and its surroundings. The day before his return to Panevėžys they have a weird meeting. A stranger comes cycling towards them and wants to tell a story. Do they know that all the Jews in Biržai are being murdered? The man tells that the German commander claimed that weapons had been found in the ghetto. In retaliation all the Jews were taken somewhere outside the city and shot. "They just killed all the Jews. All, he said. Children, babies. The German officer was walking around and shooting babies in the mothers' hands." It was unclear whether the man had participated in the massacre, but he had certainly been an eyewitness to it, most likely because he had been ordered to keep watch. "He described the execution in great detail." When they shot the babies, he left. He couldn't bear to face that.

The boys are shocked, but when Gureckas arrives in Panevėžys the next day, he learns that the mass executions are taking place everywhere. Not only in Lithuania, but also in Latvia. When a German detachment arrives with all kinds of excavators they know enough. In Panevėžys too they will murder the Jews from the ghetto set up immediately after the invasion: "... because we knew what happened in Biržai." Sunday was supposed to be the day of the killings; everyone was secretly talking about it. It was only the Bishop of Panevėžys who dared to speak out openly against it. In anticipation, he excommunicated everyone who would get involved. The Germans placed him under house arrest. Some friends who had joined the auxiliary forces guarding the ghetto fled. They were not punished for it, for there were enough volunteers who wanted to assist the Germans.

Navazelskis, with the caution that I now can recognize from her: "So, in other words, those Lithuanians who did participate — "

"Did willingly." Gureckas completes her sentence without hesitation.

Yet Gureckas does not have the date of the massacre ready either. Even the month is not clear to him. Navazelskis is leading him to the right date. The memories are no less keen.

"The day when the executions started was somehow very strange. Nobody was talking, people just didn't talk. [...] I went to visit my friend, who lived near the street where the road was leading toward Pajuostė where the executions were taking place. And the trucks full of — of Jews, I suppose, full of people who were just going that direction."

"Did you see this?" Navazelskis asks.

"Yes. And [...] we just looked, and didn't say anything. Didn't say anything because what — what can you say? What can you say?"

Navazelskis seems to be holding her breath for a moment. "So, it's like the whole city knows."

"Yes."

"The whole city knows."

"Oh yeah, the whole city knew, definitely. And the reaction was horrified, horrified. [...] There [...] have been people who approved. After all, there were people who participated. But generally [...] you can see that everybody's kind of like paralyzed from horror."

A few weeks later, Gureckas and his friends visit a girlfriend of one of them who lives on a farm near the execution site. The girl didn't see anything, as her father hid her that day from the Germans and Lithuanians walking in and out in search of water and vodka. The boys do not have the courage to go to the place of doom, but they are told details they already know from Biržai: "At the end of the execution it looked like they became insane. They were drinking vodka, complaining that they cannot get drunk, no matter how much vodka they drink."

Navazelskis asks how many Jews lived in Panevėžys.

"7,000 – 8,000."

"And in Biržai?" she asks, as if she foresaw Casper's investigation.

"Less. Considerably less, [...] because the city is much smaller."

When Navazelskis inquires whether he had heard about other massacres in the countryside, he follows with a self-confident "Yeah, yeah." Everyone was obsessed with the subject, he recounts, they couldn't stop talking about it, like it needed to get out, they were still in shock: "That's why they brought up the subject, they just – just couldn't – couldn't hold, they just wanted to – to – to – to speak about it."

In the recollection of Gureckas, the mass murder of the Jews in Panevėžys and Biržai was the talk of the town in mid-1941. Mekas remembers that it was not talked about at all, certainly not among the peasants, for the simple reason that they keep silent about that which cannot be talked about. Two memories, of two contemporaries, one a city boy, the other a farmer's son, both present in the surroundings of Biržai at the time of the massacre. Gureckas was not a direct eyewitness, but has heard enough to evoke gruesome details, even if they may have crept into his memory as tropes from what he later had learned about the Holocaust (the story of the executioners complaining that they failed to get drunk is such a recurring detail). Mekas, on only one occasion revealing that he had seen with his own eyes how babies were killed with bayonets, remembers seventy-seven years later nothing but the bagels that his mother could no longer buy.

I try to imagine Biržai after the massacre. The silence around the synagogue on Sabbath, the empty shelves in the shops, the stagnant production plants, and the deserted houses. As I walk through the street where I live in Amsterdam, I pass several "stumbling stones," small copper plaques anchored in the sidewalk to commemorate Jewish residents who were deported to be murdered in Auschwitz, Bergen-Belsen, Sobibor. In the pavement of the Merwede Square, the little park my street leads to, is one of the most famous. Anne Frank was living there at number 37, before the family went into hiding in the Secret Annex on the Prinsengracht.

If I had been living then and had lived in this neighborhood, would I have missed her and her family after they went into hiding? In the four streets leading to the Merwede Square, 2,420 of the 5,420 residents were Jewish — after the deportations almost half of the houses must have been unoccupied.

That couldn't have escaped me. The bakery that sold matsos for Pesach every year was empty. The nearest streetcar stop was hardly used. In the park flooded with a summer sun, no more children were playing, including the girl with the black, curly hair.

But did my remaining neighbors from back then talk about this? Who emptied the houses that were left behind? Could I have looked past that? Or were they silent, like my family kept silent about the Salomons at the end of the street, just like Mekas's peasant family did about the massacre in the forest of Astravas? In Amsterdam, too, people looked away en masse when the long queues were forming in front of the Hollandse Schouwburg, or, closer to my current home, the Jewish inhabitants of my neighborhood were driven together on the lawn in front of the Berlage-skyscraper, after the war triumphantly called the Victory Square, where Square of Shame might have been closer to the truth.

When I was thinking about those empty houses, I tried to imagine what Casper knew about Biržai when he did his research on Mekas. It turns out to be surprisingly easy to form a picture of this through the enormous database that the Internet brings into my study. Without having to travel to libraries or archives myself, I have the history of life in Biržai and the role the Jews played in it at my fingertips. I start, as Casper must have started, with just sweeping together some facts, general facts that sound plausible to me — it's the right footnotes that give you that certainty — and I make an attempt to summarize them.

The first Jews settled in the small town around Biržai Castle as early as the sixteenth century — I see this sentence appear on my screen and I immediately recognize a figure of speech that makes me hesitate. Every historiography seeks a starting point, and it is reassuring when it dates back several centuries: the Jews were already here for a long time, it states, as if we should need that for condemning the slaughter in Biržai. How factual is a sentence like that? How factual is it about all those individuals who through their presence have colored Biržai for centuries? Can historiography escape this figure of speech at all?

I test another sentence that I distill from my notes: The Jewish population grew and shrunk, pogroms took place on the waves of time — I realize that questioning sentences like this is a dead end. It's paralyzing. I can only solve (or avoid) my clumsiness by going straight to the end of the nineteenth century. There, at least, "history" has a direct connection with the people it would affect in 1941.

By the end of the nineteenth century, the Jews of Biržai were engaged in the trade of flax and wood, ran shops and small weaving mills, or were poor and sold their wares door-to-door. According to the 1897 census, Biržai had a population of 4,413, of whom

1,255 were Roman Catholics, 581 were Protestants, and 2,510 were Jews, nearly sixty percent of the population. This percentage may explain why the pogroms that took place in Russia at that time bypassed Biržai. However, a devastating fire followed by the First World War ruined the Jewish community, and caused an emigration wave.

After World War I, in the years that Jonas Mekas grew up there and went to school, the welfare of the Jews in Biržai recovers. In the mid 1930s, thirty-six percent of the residents are Jewish. Interesting detail: they own seventy-five percent of the houses. An official population survey in 1931 showed that seventy-seven of the ninety-nine businesses located in Biržai are in the hands of Jewish owners. Most shops are Jewish, grain and flax are the monopoly of Jewish traders, as is food processing. Jews run twenty-eight of the forty-five factories. Only among restaurants and inns are Jewish owners significantly underrepresented: three out of twenty-four.

From the mid-1930s onwards, the economic situation for the Jewish community once again became dire. The Union of Lithuanian Shopkeepers "Verslas" calls for no longer buying in Jewish shops. The demand was followed. Jewish shops collapse due to debts. Anti-Semitism surely does not arrive in Lithuania with the German invasion.

The Jewish community has its own schools and cultural activities. Also their own bank. Jewish citizens have joined the volunteer fire brigade. There is a synagogue, two prayer houses, and there are charity initiatives, which suffer from the economic recession.

There's a phrase in my notes that won't let me go: "The Lithuanians lived in their alleys and the Jews in the center of the town."

When Hitler started his war in 1939, events in Biržai followed each other in quick succession. After the German invasion of Poland, many Jewish youths flee to Lithuania. The community in Biržai welcomes a number of them in a kibbutz. During the Soviet occupation that follows, most Jewish companies were nationalized and all Zionist activities banned. Mekas recalls a Jewish mayor appointed by the communists. Just before the German invasion, three Jewish families (seventeen persons in total) were deported by the Soviets from Biržai to Siberia. They shared that fate with 20,000 other Lithuanian citizens, of whom more than thirty percent were Jews.

The Germans arrive in Biržai on the 26th of June, 1941. By then the Lithuanian nationalists already have organized themselves into a militia and are identifiable by their white armbands. From day one, Jewish civilians are murdered: a doctor, a lawyer and his family. I read: "The local 'Shokhet' [Jewish butcher] was tied with his beard to the tail of a horse and then towed through the streets till his death."

One month after the Germans have taken Biržai, all Jewish citizens are forced to leave their homes and settle in a few alleys around the synagogue. Biržai also gets its ghetto. Men are randomly arrested, taken to the Jewish cemetery and shot.

On August 8, 1941, the final phase commences. The previous days, five hundred Jewish men were forced to dig ditches in the forest of Astravas, each twenty to thirty meters long and two meters wide. During the fatal Friday, between a hundred and two hundred Jews were driven in groups to the place of execution, some three and a half kilometers outside the center of Biržai. Those sad processions passed by between eleven o'clock in the morning and seven o'clock in the evening. Twenty-four hundred faces, many of which could not have been unknown to the bystanders. I suspect that also in Biržai they must have fallen silent.

There is another sentence that preoccupies me: "The murderers divided the robbed Jewish property among themselves, only giving expensive items to the Germans, after which they returned to the town singing."

It's awkward to copy these kinds of notes. As well as looking at the group portrait of the Jewish kindergarten, made in 1939. Thirty-one boys and girls, all not older than four or five, and their teacher. Sailors' suits, crisp collars, neat dresses, blazers, white knee socks and tights – all of them dressed up that morning with the prospect of a class photo.

Or the group photo that the members of the Zionist youth movement Hashomer-Hatsair proudly had taken. Someone added their names: Gita Vishkin, Esther Gude, Yankelevitz, Sheine Roznikovitz, Bilhah Nakhumovitz, Itke Moril, Hinda Shakhar, Nahum Levitas, Tsivyah Vishkin, Zundl Fin. Confident, determined youngsters in warm winter coats. Sheine Roznikovitz knows how to look seductively into the lens, a dark glance that the men around her must have been impressed by.

Or the cheerfully toasting Sherman family and their friends, twenty-one of them crammed together in the narrow living room around a festively set table.

Did Mekas know them? The various ethnic and religious communities hardly mixed, that's well known. Yet Mekas knew Jews, like a writer who lent him his books and even took him to the synagogue. Or the shopkeepers from whom his family bought their groceries and the craftsmen who repaired his father's tools. Mekas does not remember a specific Jewish quarter in Biržai. The shops of Jewish owners were scattered all over the town. Mekas worked for some time in a pharmacy opposite a Jewish school, possibly in the summer of the massacre.

It's hard to imagine that after that fatal Friday, the small town didn't feel like a ghost town. Or had the Lithuanians moved out of their alleys to the center of town overnight, freed from rental obligations to the Jewish owners of their homes?

It is tempting to turn to the possibilities of fiction to fill in the gaps. At times, only imagination is capable of providing a story with truth. With details that are evoked by memories of other events. No matter how strongly supported by facts, only when the imagination makes a novel out of history can it come to life. No historian can escape this. Casper, too, must have imagined the empty Biržai. And it must have given him an idea of plausibility: such a void does not escape you. I'm inclined to follow him in this. No matter how brief, at some point Biržai looked like an abandoned city. Not having a memory of that is strange. Very strange?

trauma

Practically everyone I speak about my research on Mekas suggests at some point the possibility of "repression": Mekas has, whether consciously or not, banned the events in the forest of Astravas from his active memory and stored them in a part of his brain where they can't trouble him. It has been a traumatic experience, and he has tried to forget it for good. So far, I too have used metaphors that play with this thought and suggested that Mekas may have stored the event in a "sealed compartment" of his mind. The use of such a compartment is seen by almost everyone I ask as a self-evident skill of ours.

In a lucid chapter in *Forgetting*, Dutch memory

scholar Douwe Draaisma claims that surveys show that even the vast majority of psychologists and psychiatrists are convinced of the possibility of repression. This is remarkable, because no psychological research has yet been able to prove experimentally that the human mind can actually do this. In fact, since the 1990s, there have been many more indications that events that we label as traumatic are not at all inclined to let themselves be stored away and forgotten by us. In the phrasing of Draaisma: "What traumas seem to demand of memory is their recurrence rather than their repression."

Paradoxically, this is also a thought that almost everyone will recognize and endorse. The diagnosis Post Traumatic Stress Disorder (PTSD) has become an integral part of our vocabulary after the wars in Iraq and everything that followed. Natural disasters, peace missions, refugees' stories, terrorist attacks, rapes, violent crimes, no one is surprised if those involved are haunted afterwards by anxiety syndromes, nightmares, obsessive-compulsive neurosis or uncontrollable loss of social inhibitions. In our daily language, traumatic events now qualify just as easily for a fleetingly formulated diagnosis of "PTSD" as for the diagnosis of "repression." We use what suits us best.

If we stick to "repression" (when it comes to Mekas, in my mini-questionnaire the most often suggested), it is striking that there is at least something half-hearted in our perception of it. After all, we know that someone is repressing something because he or she is conveying signals that reveal the existence of the repressed event to us. Hence, even when the forgotten event is repressed, it knocks on the door. Not with a fist or loudly, as we assume with PTSD, but secretly or via a detour. Whoever pays close attention will pick up the signals and see their revealing meaning.

Freud was a master of using circular reasoning to impose his interpretation upon those signals. Draaisma meticulously discusses "the case study of Dora," a classic in Freudian analysis. When Dora plays on Freud's divan with her little purse, constantly clicking it open and letting her finger slide into it, he interprets it as an unconscious desire to masturbate. He teaches future psychoanalysts that who is silent with his lips, chats with his fingertips. An instruction that has been picked up widely. Virtually every novelist, screenwriter or playwright makes use of it, without having to fall back on Freudian jargon. Whoever writes a story plants symptoms in his characters that the reader or viewer is expected to recognize and interpret.

Anti-Freudians may not like to hear it, but audiences are very adept at recognizing patterns such as Freud has described. A slip of the tongue, stammering, tics, evasive behavior, subtext, we know how to use them flawlessly to interpret the personalities or actions of characters — it is at the heart of our dramatic arts.

Is it a problem that something that cannot be proven scientifically works so well? According to Draaisma, in psychological and psychiatric *practices* the belief in the existence of a mental disorder is just as important as the empirical confirmation or its refutation. Or, when formulated rather harshly, whoever believes in something, behaves accordingly. This applies just as much to the patient as it does to the therapist, or, for that matter, to the novelist and his reader, the filmmaker and his audience.

In the end, it doesn't seem to matter if we can correctly establish methodologically that Mekas has repressed the events in the forest of Astravas. What matters in the context of his "case" is that we lay the memory of Mekas so easily and self-evidently along that yardstick. The metaphors we use for it are generally accepted as insightful, clarifying and explanatory. Both those who defend Mekas and those who think they should criticize him equally make use of them.

In the same way, Casper is just as "agile." Where one part of his argument tries to present facts, the other part, without giving justification, makes use of interpretation techniques that one might call "Freudian" – or, less burdened – "dramaturgic." Casper reads the patient (or character) Mekas and interprets the hidden signals in his work and phrases. By identifying these signals as such, Casper plants them in the reader's mind just as an experienced novelist would. Historiography, the art of the novel and psychological interpretation merge imperceptibly.

The fact that we are hardly surprised at this shows how deeply this way of dealing with meaning is embedded in our observations. The only person who is not pleased with it in this case is Jonas Mekas. Any defense on his part is swallowed up by the glutton of interpretation, in which every signal adds up to previous ones. Once you are in the defendant's dock of repression, any defense will get you further into a jam.

"I went through horrors more unbelievable than anything I had read in the books, and it all happened right before my eyes — before my eyes the heads of children were smashed with bayonets" — I accepted Casper's interpretation of this statement in the commencement speech as a significant "slip of the tongue" of Mekas without giving it much thought. Mekas had to have seen the murder of Jewish babies with his own eyes. The fact that he didn't mention "Jewish" anywhere in that speech is only symptomatic of the process of repression. After all, anyone who withholds something is whispering a veiled confession.

As an experienced analyst (and interviewer), Casper tried to bring Mekas back to the place where the trauma must have occurred. Has he perhaps been in the forest of Astravas, he asks? It brings Mekas to a confirmation that makes Casper sound like a first, albeit half confession: "He said that he visited the killing site only a week later. — 'Just passing where they were shot — there were so many in those graves in Astravas, across, on the other side of the lake, they were almost' — he motioned with his arm as if to indicate that the graves were moving. 'You could almost smell it,' he said. 'So that's real enough!'" This is the most specific indication that Mekas saw "something" of the massacre: the outcome, the graves. He still tells it with great restraint, forced to do so, I imagine, by Casper's persistent questioning. The memory appears as an image he wants to push away, his mind's eye tries to block itself off from it.

Mekas once said in an interview that he had only made one attempt to incorporate the Holocaust into his art, in the short story "The Wolf" from 1957. Casper skillfully analyses the introduction of the wolf in the story as "a creature being beaten and tortured until it expires in a manner that seems to evoke the anti-Jewish vigilantism that occurred in Biržai in July 1941."

Casper's not satisfied with that one story. Now that he's on the path of interpretation, he's looking for Dora's little purse. Which is not difficult in Mekas's extensive oeuvre. After all, the interpreter only needs half a word, and Mekas is someone of half words and unfinished sentences: his work on paper and celluloid is a gold mine of holistic and poetic contractions. Anyone looking for "Verdichtung" ("condensation") will be richly rewarded with Mekas; it is the essence of his artistic project. He shares this with all his colleagues in experimental filmmaking: speaking the unutterable, inventing a new, tactile language for this.

Casper can hardly be blamed for searching for it, because Mekas likes to flirt with the inexpressible, and not only in his films. In 2007, Mekas published *My Night Life*, in which he reveals the dreams he has written down from August 1978 to June 1979. Those who make their dreams public inspire "Traumdeutung" ("dream interpretation").

In one of Mekas's dreams that interests Casper in particular, the office of the Film-Makers Cooperative resembles that of *The New Biržai News* at the time of the Second World War. Casper: "In the dream, police arrive and accuse Mekas's friend and fellow-Lithuanian, the artist George Maciunas, of having killed someone. But Mekas realizes that it was in fact he who had done it, and buried the body beneath the floorboards of George's Soho loft. 'I was afraid that the corpse could get out from under the floor,' Mekas wrote. 'I saw that there was a large indented hole such as I saw in Astravas over the graves of the Jews who were shot.'"

Casper doesn't need Freud to interpret this dream as an unconscious desire for a confession: Mekas has definitely seen more than just the graves. Needless to say, in Mekas's denial he recognizes a classic case of "Abwehr" ("defense").

It's no different with Mekas's poetry. Having been put on the track of interpretation by Casper, I find a treasure trove of "slips of the tongue." Like this fragment from *Daybooks 1970–72* (in the translation by Vyt Bakaitis):

Times were bad.
Now, everything
-'s gone in
        the past.

But one
pain
stuck,
from
across
the lake.

Or from the poem "A Requiem for the XXth Century," written January 3, 2000:

Scars are on our bodies, minds,
souls even,
some of us do not always sleep well
all night -- I don't -- sometimes we still
jump up, not knowing why, as horrors
linger.

Recollections of horrors that live on in Mekas, what other catastrophe could that be than the murder of the

2,400 Jews of Biržai? Or can I read the poet's words only with the knowledge that Casper has planted in me?

So far, I have assumed that Mekas wanted to forget. But not wanting to speak about something doesn't mean that the event has been intentionally erased or deleted. The sporadic "slips of the tongue" may indicate that Mekas only occasionally found the right words for it. Possibly he realized that his imagination failed to give the event the weight it deserved. Maybe we shouldn't talk about repression, but about powerlessness. Why shouldn't there be events for which there are no words — no adequate words? Wouldn't it be better to remain silent instead of wasting words that sound false, insincere?

Oddly enough, that's an idea I quickly had put aside. Interpretation is also driven by the satisfaction of the find. Dora's little purse must have pleased Freud intensely. Reading the poetry of Mekas in search of the forest of Astravas has a lot in common with that. Casper's psychoanalysis no less, but do all Mekas's "slips of the tongue" really touch the hidden core of his existence?

character

It seems that a net is closing in, as if only that one event has taken place in Mekas's life — the traumatic incident about which he prefers to remain silent. And that one episode explains to us exhaustively who he is. From Homer to Tolstoi, for the narrator it is extremely useful to characterize someone with a single trait — that way we will be able to recognize him at any moment and not forget him. But do the stylistic devices of fiction correspond with reality?

The New York Review of Books published one letter to the editor about Casper's article. Poet and art historian Barry Schwabsky stands up for Mekas. He especially criticizes the suggestive tone of the article. In defense of Mekas's sloppy memory, he also suggests the possibility of repression as a result of an unresolved trauma. Mekas is not to be held accountable for such forgetfulness, he says. People unconsciously defend themselves against traumas with a selective memory — it would do Casper honor to show more respect for that.

Casper is not impressed. In his reply, he plays a new card, which I suspect he only found after writing his article. Mekas's forgetting is not at all, as Schwabsky suggests, subconscious or involuntary: "... in April, in London, Hans Ulrich Obrist asked Mekas at a public interview about the historian Eric Hobsbawm's directive for the 'need to protest against forgetting.' Mekas interrupted the question to declare, 'My dream is that humanity someday would totally lose all memory. So there wouldn't be always remembering who did what to my nation, to me.'" Casper concludes: "This suggests to me that Mekas's memory is not only selective but ideologically so." In the epic of Casper, Mekas is invariably "the Great Forgetful." Every snippet of the "Mekas-character" reminds him of this.

Do we really have to take Mekas's plea for total oblivion that seriously? It often strikes me that Casper has little feeling for the provocative, playful, confrontational, irresponsible and immature nature of Mekas's statements. Certainly in his public appearances Mekas likes to seek the atmosphere of the Fluxus art movement, such as he admired in the performances of his friend and fellow Lithuanian, George Maciunas.

In the early 1960s, notorious enfant terrible Maciunas turned the New York art scene upside down with neo-Dadaist events — absurdist performances, ready-mades, wry humor and the assertion that every form of signification was bankrupt. These were Fluxus vehicles of attack. Apart from a firm belief in the provocation, the "movement" proclaimed by Maciunas was difficult to capture in definitions. It was anti-art that would decisively influence artists as diverse as Yoko Ono, Nam June Paik, and in Europe, Joseph Beuys.

When I worked on this book, I was able to see first hand what such a Fluxus performance meant. Prior to the screening of *George — The Story of George Maciunas and Fluxus* at the Amsterdam Eye Filmmuseum, director and Maciunas biographer

Jeffrey Perkins presented his “Fluxus Butthead” performance. Perkins first had his head shaved in public, then bent over and started a small film projector. On his shiny head he projected *Bottoms*, a short film in which Yoko Ono in 1966 portrayed her friends’ naked buttocks in black and white. The performance unfolded in an almost devout silence, which certainly contributed to the alienating tension. Is this really happening, I was constantly wondering? Are we really watching this in a sold-out movie theatre?

Maciunas was thirteen years old when he and his family fled Lithuania from the advancing Red Army to Germany. They emigrated to the United States in 1948. In the small Lithuanian exile community it was not surprising that Mekas and he made friends. Until the premature death of Maciunas in 1978, their lives remained connected. Maciunas would certainly have been pleased with Mekas’s brash statement on forgetting — provocation was his raison d’être.

The public interview in London took place in April 2018, just two months before the publication of Casper’s article. It can be viewed on the Internet. Obrist, director of the Serpentine Gallery, presents Mekas as a Zen master of the avant-garde, whose wisdoms he notes eagerly. Mekas feels at ease on familiar ground and enjoys that status.

The interview precedes a screening of *Out-Takes from the Life of a Happy Man* from 2012. Out-takes is film-editor jargon for shots that don't make the final cut. Mekas proclaims that there are no rejected or unusable shots to him. He saves everything he films, stores the rolls of film side by side on a shelf to make use of when it suits him. That's why his film with "old" shots is not about the past, but about the present, because it's screening, after all, takes place right now. "I am totally disinterested in the past," he explains to the audience. All his work stems from a sense of movement. *Panta rhei* is the adage the ancient Greeks already taught us, everything flows, and that flow inevitably brings Mekas into an ever present: the moment is the only thing that counts. A real Fluxus idea: art never exists longer than the moment of its performance.

It seems a perfect upbeat to his plea for total amnesia, but Mekas is not a philosopher looking for a coherent, argumentative discourse. He has his own agenda and interrupts the interview to tell the audience a story. Recently he met a dog in a subway station in New York. More precisely "an angry dog," who spoke to him. Mekas fumbles out of his bag a mask of a fearsome looking sheepdog, the tongue out of his mouth, the teeth bare. He pulls the mask over his head and starts, as the dog, a long lamentation.

Does Mekas realize how museums these days are dealing with famous film works, the dog asks him at the subway station. MOMA, for example, which he recently visited, displayed the *Screen Tests* that Andy

Warhol filmed of his friends between 1964 and 1966 on video. Video! Didn't the museum know that these tests were shot on film? When he inquired about it, the museum's defense was that screening them on film would be too expensive. The same was the case, the dog continued, with the films of Joseph Cornell, who had never heard of video and would certainly not have screened his films in that way. The dog, now that it's in the mood for criticizing, is also sincerely angry with the large galleries that have squeezed the little ones out of the art world. Everything must be big these days, he grumbles, even the paintings.

Obrist films the Dadaist spectacle with his telephone, no doubt to transmit it via Twitter, Instagram or Facebook. The audience loves it and laughs greedily, although no one seems to realize that Mekas's plea for the original film material of Andy Warhol and Joseph Cornell is a plea for the "pure" memory. The present is apparently not the only thing that matters after all. The past does deserve our respect, the dog claims, which the obsessive archivist who Mekas is, will not easily contradict.

Obrist follows up on that thought. He shows the public a new book by Mekas, *Conversations with Filmmakers*: interviews with sixty filmmakers that he made between 1958 and 1975 mainly for *The Village Voice*. Not just celebrities like Agnes Varda and Pier Paolo Pasolini, says Obrist, but also filmmakers who are now almost forgotten. To get to the quote so eagerly picked up by Casper.

Referring to Hobsbawn, Obrist suggests that Mekas will undoubtedly endorse his plea for remembrance. Mekas is still too much in the Fluxus mood of his dog performance to just acknowledge that. No, he's interrupting Obrist fiercely, he's on the contrary fantasizing that mankind will lose its memory completely! The audience still thinks the angry dog is speaking and laughs exuberantly. What sounds disconnected from this context as a self-assured, ideologically driven statement, can be recognized in reality as an ordinary provocation, the Dadaist exclamation by an anti-artist.

The psychoanalytic historian can, of course, take this as a slip of the tongue, as a signal from the unconscious. The gibberish in which Mekas subsequently loses himself when he tries to substantiate his thesis would corroborate this. But then, I suddenly hear some words in his response that clarify his argument: "revenge" and "a thousand years." What I think Mekas, in his reeling and stuttering, tries to say is that in the name of history, people and nations are still making each other's lives miserable. This could be put to an end if we at least allowed ourselves to let oblivion do its work.

I think it echoes David Rieff's *In Praise of Forgetting: Historical Memory and Its Ironies* (2016), in which the journalist concludes that many of the wars he has covered were waged under the pretext of avenging an injustice from a distant past. The Serbs invoked the conquest of Constantinople by the Muslim Ottomans in 1453 (which they spoke of as if it had taken place yesterday) in the 1990s to justify the massacre of Muslims in Bosnia. Rieff was there, and it led him to address the irony of historical memory in a polemical and provocative book. Forgetting is sometimes wiser (and healthier) than the endless racking up of historical events to provide the present with arguments to go on the warpath. Those who do not want to forget often abuse the past to justify their questionable role in the present, Rieff argues. Mekas seems to have picked up on that thought – and is the clumsy messenger of it in London.

Is it strange to refer to David Rieff all of a sudden?

Not when you realize that Rieff is the son of Susan Sontag, with whom Mekas has been friends since the sixties. Sontag used to drag her son, still at a young age, to the film performances of Mekas and his friends. He was the kid who was put to sleep on his mother's coat while she rushed to the reception, party or gallery opening.

How such friendship worked, Mekas captures in an episode of his *365 Day Project* (a proto-vlog from 2003). In it he shows a rendezvous from October 2001. Sontag and the Hungarian cult director Béla Tarr chat at the kitchen table. Sontag asks Tarr if he makes use of the fairly new phenomenon of email. Tarr, famous for robust, bleak, rainy film scenes without an end, doesn't want to hear anything of it. Mekas's camera first watches an amused Tarr and then a very relaxed Sontag. She says that she has more young than elderly friends and in order to keep in touch with them she has given in to email. Outside the frame, Mekas grumbles that he already has enough trouble keeping up with his paper mail.

This is the "Mekas mood": two celebrities at his table chatting a bit. He has often recorded these situations in his home movies, usually without sound, leaving the "conversation" to the imagination of the viewer. I think they give an insight into how Mekas gets his ideas: friends among each other, skimming the subjects of the day entertainingly but not too deeply.

Mekas ideas arise ad hoc and non-committal, is my impression. That may sound bold, as if I don't want to take him seriously. I think "serious" is not the right word for someone who mainly wants to "disrupt." I don't see an ideologue that you should want to pinpoint on the consistency of his words. What I see is a Fluxus artist who, without the slightest embarrassment, rings bells with intentionally misunderstood clappers. Mekas is first of all performance, only secondly argument or idea. His admirers have appointed him as an oracle, and he enjoys that role. He gets away with it because he sounds funny, cheeky, and provocative. Any film festival wishes itself such a guest.

Should we then not take that sentence about the children's heads crushed by bayonets from 1966, which put Casper on the trail of Mekas's trauma, seriously either?

Being Dutch, I'm not really familiar with the tradition of the commencement speech, although I have seen enough clips of famous celebration orators and a shower of hundreds of caps to understand that it's an honor to address the new graduates. It is a moment of optimism; guiding young people with good advice to the gateway of a new life. I tracked the full text on the website of the Philadelphia College of Art and read that Mekas had shown himself at his best in that respect. It was the eve of the "Summer of Love" and Mekas wanted the new generation to believe that a glorious, loving future awaited them, in which they could make a break with a past of war, for which his generation had been responsible.

It's a wide-ranging vision of the future, flower power in the making, but as in any text or film by his hand, Mekas shifts the focus to himself. On closer inspection, the lecture can also be read as a victory speech over trauma. Mekas needs the "confession" about the children's heads for that, although you have to pay the utmost attention to highlight the sentence within the full text.

This is the full passage: "There was a time, when I was sixteen or seventeen, when I was idealistic and believed that the world would change in my own lifetime. I read about all the suffering of man, wars and misery that took place in the past centuries. And I somehow believed that in my own lifetime all this would change. I had faith in the progress of man, in the goodness of man. And then came the war, and I went through horrors more unbelievable than anything I had read in the books, and it all happened right before my eyes— before my eyes the heads of children were smashed with bayonets. And this was done by my generation. And it's still being done today, in Vietnam, by my generation. It's done all over the world, by my generation. Everything that I believed in shook to the foundations — all my idealism, and my faith in the goodness of man and progress of man; all was shattered. My mind went to pieces. I went through a terrible time. Somehow, I managed to keep myself together. But, really, I wasn't one piece any longer; I was one thousand painful pieces."

Pull that one sentence out of this paragraph, which I deliberately did not highlight, and you do have your confession. Casper eagerly isolates it. And presents it as a dry fact. What disappears then is that the text is mainly about crushed idealism and the path Mekas had to take in order to regain his faith in it. It was his film work that brought him relief.

Mekas recounts that after seeing his experimental films, many people ask him when he is going to make a real movie. By this they mean films such as Hollywood makes them. Films in which Mekas believes you can't find real people. The small underground films, on the other hand, made by himself and his friends, promises the spectator a home: "We want to remind him that there is such a thing as home, where he can be, once and a while, alone and with himself and with a few that he loves close to him, and be with himself and his soul — that's the meaning of the home movie, the private visions of our movies."

Home movies are a home, even if they are made of celluloid, even if they are just projections of shadows on a screen. The heartbeat of the creators can be heard in them. They give the earth warmth. These small, unambitious films have a healing power. Certainly for Mekas, he confesses. They have forged back together the thousand pieces into which he had fallen apart: "After fifteen years of disillusionment, slowly, during the last few months, I have gained again the belief and trust in man, and the knowledge that this is the generation that is building the bridge from horror to light."

Future vision and the defeat of a personal trauma are blending together. The experimental, highly personal home movies, which many spectators don't acknowledge as "real movies," helped him to do so. They have given him a home. Cinema is good, isn't it?

The memory of bayonets crushing children's heads doesn't seem to me to have been a "slip of the tongue," not a signal that secretively escaped from a locked compartment. Mekas was able to retrieve it in his speech, because it was an image he had overcome with his films. Paradoxically, it also made it possible to forget that image as well. Because it lay – at last – behind him. The massacre in the forest of Astravas was after 1966 not, I believe, hidden in a *secret* compartment, but kept in a highly personal *sealed* compartment. Deliberately forgotten to be able to start again, with a clean slate. Not ideologically motivated, but out of personal necessity.

loyalty

When I re-read my interpretation of the commencement speech, it feels like an attempt to put Mekas back on the safe side of moral judgment. Am I seeking that relief? I realize that I would still prefer to simply take Mekas at his word. Even if his memory fails him, I don't see why that should indicate bad intentions. Why would there be deceitful intentions behind that? That may be a naive point of view (I'm no investigative journalist), but as long as I don't have the impression that Mekas has committed explicit crimes, I'd rather not trade my benevolence for suspicion. If this is the life Mekas wants to remember, let it *be* his life. I have the same attitude towards my friends, the people I love. The last thing I want is to embarrass the Mekas I admire.

Or am I afraid to embarrass myself? My attitude, I realize, is not one of truth-finding, but of loyalty: I don't want to lose the trust I placed in Mekas as an adolescent cinephile. Believing in someone whose reputation is publicly shattered evokes shame. How have I ever been able to believe in this person? What have I overlooked that others have seen? I prefer to dodge those questions. It may explain my desire to condone: not the person who is guilty, but the circumstances that led him to his actions and his silence.

This is not Casper's attitude, or that of any journalist or historian. The approach of historiography is to find the truth: how did it happen and what were the intentions? If that embarrasses certain people, so be it. The historian wants to do justice to history, which is where his loyalty lies. There is no room for shame, or for loyalty to a person. Casper believes in the inviolability of the facts. These precede his judgment. To be more precise, they make his judgment inevitable. Put the facts together, and the conclusion is there for the taking. In the email Casper wrote to me it sounds like this: "Mekas certainly lied to me, Ina [Navazelskis] and other people about his past."

It is a crystal clear conclusion. With this, Casper in no way denies the complexity of Mekas's memory: "This doesn't mean he didn't also dissociate, willfully forget, intentionally obscure, come to believe his own lies, or some combination of these." To which he unexpectedly adds: "At the same time, much of what he said is truthful." Casper sees it as his task as a historian to disentangle truth and lie in Mekas's memory. On the basis of facts. But how hard are these facts?

To tackle this question, I want to return once more to the story of the flight. Mekas claims that he tried to travel to Vienna because he was afraid of being exposed by the Germans as the one who typed out BBC radio messages for illegal distribution. His flight is one for the Nazis — to German territory (in which, of course, the ambiguity lies). According to Casper, this representation is not plausible. The documents show that the Germans had stopped arresting Lithuanian citizens weeks before the flight.

Casper's underlying suggestion is that Mekas's involvement in the collaborationist magazines is the real reason for his flight. He is afraid of the Red Army's advance. He flees, together with the Germans, from the Soviets. The credibility thereof is given to Casper by the chairman of the subcommittee of the Lithuanian scientific research group that focuses on the role of the Nazis in Lithuania, an important keeper of the current historical paradigm: "The Lithuanian-American historian Saulius Sužiedėlis told me that, to his knowledge, 'fleeing the Nazis in 1944' didn't conform to 'the experience of ninety-nine percent of the people' who left Lithuania then — to escape the Soviets."

For the plausibility of Mekas's story, only one percent remains. It indeed sounds like very little, but how many refugees were there in absolute numbers that deviated from the norm? Isn't it the beauty of individual human lives that they can be "exceptional"? Casper does not believe in stories too good to be true. To him, Mekas's private story is not in line with the general trend described on the basis of documents (the German occupiers stopped their arrests) and the accumulation of testimonies from other refugees. He shifts the burden of proof to Mekas — who only has his memory.

Mekas, of course, could have shrugged his shoulders. Yes, he fled from the Soviets and Germany was the only option — what's wrong with that? It would have been the simple solution. But Mekas insists on how it happened according to him, which is less clear-cut than how Casper thinks it happened. And not in sync with the ninety-nine percent of his fellow countrymen who were also fleeing.

When I ask Ina Navazelskis how she judges the flight story, she is reluctant. She represents the oral history project of the USHMM, and it is not her role to be judgmental. Still, she wants to say something about it in the Skype interview. She remembers Mekas's story about what led to the flight as one of the most emotional moments of the interview. It has made an impression on her. I recognize what she says. If there's one memory that emotionally moves Mekas in the six hours with Navazelskis, it's this one. The story of the flight gets an extra dimension. Moreover, Mekas adds a few important details that I didn't know from earlier versions.

Firstly, he makes his role in the resistance smaller than the impression I had before. Mekas has only one liaison in the Lithuanian underground, someone he only knew by sight as a pupil in a class lower than his own. The man brings him the written notes he has to type out and picks them up two days later. It's a routine they maintain for several years, and it's Mekas's contribution to the Lithuanian resistance movement. Then follows the often-told story of the stolen typewriter, which was hidden under a pile of firewood outside the house. But from here the story suddenly becomes more grim than I knew it — and more poignant. When, after the theft, Mekas can't hand over the promised sheets, the resistance man panics and pulls out his gun and points it at Mekas. "You know what this means" he snarls at him with a pinched voice, "this could be your end." The Germans are in search of the typewriter, Mekas also knows, they have discussed this with each other, after all. Still with the gun pointed at him the contact person leaves no doubt about what he expects from Mekas: he has to disappear, immediately.

Mekas relives the event, the decisive turn in his life, with wet eyes. It's as if he feels the gun still pointed at him, he doesn't trust the trembling hands of the resistance fighter, and realizes that the child's play is over for good. The "real" war has fallen into his house – lines of verse and the knowledge of spelling no longer matter.

Is Mekas acting? Ideating? True, it sounds like a scene from a B-movie in contrasting black and white. Navazelskis doesn't want to assess the story that way. She observes the emotion, the ferocity with which the memory "returns." Whatever happened in reality, for Mekas this is the emotionally charged truth. The emotion has become the event.

Mekas must have told Casper his flight story in a similar manner. Casper thinks the story should be written out differently. It doesn't fit in with the general story of ninety-nine percent of the refugees from Lithuania in 1944. For Casper, this is sufficient reason not to believe Mekas's story, by which he sets aside not only the event, but also the underlying emotion.

It's the struggle of this essay in a nutshell. Do I want to believe the individual emotion, or do I attach more value to historical probability? Do I believe Mekas? Or do I believe Casper? I constantly have the feeling that those two positions are diametrically opposed. For the historian, there seems to be little more to it than sticking rigidly to the general story – and sacrifice personal emotion accordingly. I myself am inclined to go along with the individual story, and to believe the personal. Are the two really irreconcilable?

*

There is again a parallel story, but this time of a historian, which has helped me to understand better the tension between those two positions.

In 1989, Sheila Fitzpatrick sits in the plane next to a man who begins a chat with her. During the flight the two fall in love. Michael Danos and Fitzpatrick get married. Ten years later, her great love dies from the effects of a stroke. It takes six years before she and his oldest daughter from a previous marriage open a box he left for them. They find letters, diaries and photographs of both Michael and his mother Olga, in which their history from just before, during and immediately after the Second World War in Latvia, Germany and the United States can be read in detail. It is as if she gets her beloved back, even though it is from a period in which she did not yet know him. Michael was born as Mischka (Misha for his loved ones) in Riga, in 1922, the same year as Jonas Mekas in neighboring Lithuania.

The documents are an emotional treasure that personally mean a lot to Fitzpatrick, but she is also a historian, with several renowned studies of the Soviet Union and Stalinism to her name. It has taught her, she writes, to distrust personal documents. The historian, she believes, must describe and interpret broader truths about collective experiences. Individuals too often behave like deviant troublemakers (my wording): "Once you have real individual people in your sights, you constantly notice anomalies, divergences from expected norms. [...] Individuals are not statistical averages." In her late husband, she recognizes such a nuisance, who puzzles her more than that he provides her with answers that confirm the "expected standards."

It takes Fitzpatrick until 2017 to turn the box into a story. *Mischka's War: A Story of Survival from War-Torn Europe to New York* is a tribute to her beloved, his individual story and that of his mother. A family memoir written in commission, albeit not after she has checked every snippet with her sharp eye for what archives can confirm or contradict. This has made her realize, she confesses, how big the differences are between the *personal biographer* and the *impersonal historian* she has been up to now. She is constantly wondering whether she is the loving wife who writes, or the one who once imposed the "historian's Hippocratic oath" on herself: "... don't leave things out because you don't like them." Even for her Misha, she doesn't want to break that oath, even though she sometimes wakes up at night wondering if she shouldn't have protected him better.

As a spouse, she doesn't like how he dealt with the women in his life when he was young. How he coolly rejects them in short letters, after he has previously made them fall head over heels in love with him. In his diary he can be pompous, like all teenagers and adolescents who like to read philosophical wisdom in their immature thoughts. She doesn't recognize the dry romantic she has fallen for.

What she does recognize is a coming of age in the most unwelcome circumstances imaginable: the lives of Mischka, his family and compatriots are the unpredictable playthings of two totalitarian, criminal superpowers. Fitzpatrick knows this history like no other; it is her area of expertise as a historian. The long-term perspective is very clear to her: a history of crimes, terror, bureaucracy, the fate of victims, the Holocaust. Moreover, it annoys her that in Mischka's letters and diaries she hears "... some rather loud silences about the Jewish question and Nazism." Which, if I may pose as a historian for a moment, I am also beginning to recognize as "a statistical average" that applied to many during the Second World War.

Mischka is raised in a bourgeois family: his father is an opera singer; his mother, a charming seductress who adores her son. His great passion is physics; he dreams of one day studying at a German university. As an adolescent, he enjoys typical city pleasures and has girlfriends. During the occupation by the Germans (a history similar to that of Lithuania), Olga, his mother, uses her charms to keep her sewing work-
shop running, among other things by making straw slippers for the German army. Jews from the ghetto are given permission to work for her.

It is that light scent of collaboration that worries

Fitzpatrick. But while Casper in his analysis of Mekas's actions gives way to moral dismay, Fitzpatrick tries to fathom the private lives of Mischka and Olga. She wants to understand with a sense for "anomalies and deviations" the sacrifices it takes to survive in conditions of war and totalitarian occupation without letting the moral compass run wild.

Olga and the Jews is such a complex story. She is angling for orders from the German army (she even travels to Prague for it) and simultaneously offers Jews employed by her the chance to escape the ghetto. One person in particular succeeds, because after the war, when she hopes penniless in Germany to emigrate to the United States, a Jewish refugee who has made the crossing earlier is willing to act as a sponsor for her. Olga saved his life, he claims. Such an act was not without danger. Mary, Olga's sister, was hiding Jews in her apartment until a neighbor betrays her. The Germans arrested her in 1943. She was deported to Ravensbrück, which she miraculously survived.

Olga is a philanderer who knows how to manipulate officers, who easily fall in love with her, as well as Germans in occupied Latvia and English and Americans in Germany after the war. All this always for her own benefit and that of her children, and if it turned out that way, for the benefit of her Jewish workers. She also knows what awaits the Jews if she does not come to their aid. The Riga ghetto is used to "accommodate" Jews from neighboring countries. To make room for this, as in a kind of transfer station, the massacres continued throughout the war.

What this implies, Mischka understands through an experience that will have a decisive impact on his life. Fitzpatrick describes the event in detail, not least because it helps her to fathom the character of her beloved. Throughout their marriage, he has written her long emails about his life before they met. In one of those "musings," as he calls them, he remembers Easter Sunday of 1943.

Winter is extreme that year, and Mischka goes skiing, not far from Riga. He leaves the busy slopes and skis to a ridge he never has been to before. There he is surprised by a long parade of people, whole families on their way in a relaxed procession. Curious, he joins them and follows the track flattened by heavy vehicles. At the top of the hill, a mass grave of ten by ten meters and more than six meters deep has been dug out, completely filled with corpses, partly covered with calcium chlorate.

"So that was the Jews' graveyard."

He now sees that other hilltops have already been covered with fresh earth. On a nearby hill another pit is being dug.

He flees in shock, overwhelmed by fear and a "mental-emotional short-circuit." What keeps him busy on his way home is what drives his compatriots to visit these graves: "What is in their mind, taking the children to drink in the horror? How is it that this is a Sunday afternoon enjoyment?"

At home, to his surprise, both parents know about the graves.

Misha has always experienced this knowledge as "unbearable" ever since, he confesses to Fitzpatrick. It has cut him off from certain parts of himself, as he calls it. He was no longer able to find the emotional depth of Beethoven's "Mondscheinsonate" in himself when he played the piano. Forty years later, he still did not manage to open the door to the feeling of it.

It reveals something about her husband that Fitzpatrick had never been able to understand before. She often wondered why her loving Misha was such a "bad" witness. He listened and watched events "without being drawn in." He had never spoken to her about the mass grave before. Could she have blamed him for that? Could she have challenged him, as Casper criticized Mekas, as a witness who "eluded his responsibility"? She opts to emphasize how the "sight of the mass grave" emotionally threw Misha's life, or at least part of it, into a lockdown. It is his major, unspoken trauma, with which she too, without being able to really untangle it, had to live.

The admirable thing about Fitzpatrick, or at least when I try to imagine writing my beloved's memoir myself, is that she doesn't lose her suspicion — and at the same time puts all her considerable skills as an archival researcher to work for Mischka's story as a young man.

Misha once told her that in April 1944 (about two months prior to Mekas), he had traveled to Germany as an "exchange student." He received a scholarship to study physics, which would eventually bring him to Vienna (what Mekas failed to do). The story took Fitzpatrick's breath away; she had difficulty believing it. Traveling freely to Germany seemed to her a sign of collaboration, or at least of inappropriate support from Olga's German officer friends. Her intuition as a historian puts her on the side of the ninety-nine percent option.

The story is still open-ended when Misha dies, but she cannot omit it from her book. She has already given up clarifying the matter when she accidentally discovers in an "obscure German scholarly monograph" that there really was such an exchange program between Germany and the Baltic States during the Second World War. Misha even turned out to have remembered the exact year of its inception.

The program could exist because the Baltic people scored high in the racial hierarchy of the Nazis. Germanization of these peoples had to be pursued, and this meant privileges that were unthinkable for Poles, for example, let alone Jews. Only about a hundred students made use of it. For Mischka, it was an extraordinary opportunity: he was able to realize his dream of studying physics and at the same time avoid military service, which would have put him on the Eastern Front.

Does it also sound less strange now that Mekas's uncle (who had an academic background and was a vicar) came up with the idea of presenting the flight to Germany as a trip to a university study and that he provided the right papers for that? If such an exchange program actually existed, then it was a clever cover-up, which might have worked well two months earlier. I've emailed Casper twice about the story in *Mischka's War*, but he hasn't responded. I deduce from that that he saw no reason to investigate the one percent option.

The relief of biographer Fitzpatrick when she discovers that the exchange program really did exist indicates how much she wanted to save her beloved from the stain of Nazi sympathies. Fitzpatrick can offer a helping hand to the young man Misha once was. Misha would have wondered about that. There was no need for a helping hand — what could he have done wrong? Here too I am beginning to recognize a "historical average": Michael Danos was "unaware" of any wrongdoing — it simply doesn't occur to him —, which I imagine could evoke Casper's ire.

Mischka Danos, in his twenties, sought his way through the labyrinth of various political powers without too many ideological considerations. He had witnessed how the Soviets operated: ideologically unrelenting and at the same time frighteningly unpredictable. Under a regime like that, he never wanted to live again anyway. The ease with which he thought he could make use of the exchange program shows how flexible his principles were. His passion for physics was stronger than his contempt for Nazism or the German war machine. Nazi Germany gave him the opportunity to devote himself to science. Nowhere was physics practiced at a higher level than in Germany. In his eyes, a scientific study was free of ideology, which tells us something about his positivist belief in science — and his political naivety, for that matter.

Would Casper have let Michael Danos get away with the characterization "naive"? Fitzpatrick could not accept her beloved's choice between two evils (studying in the perfidious Germany or staying in Estonia to become a Soviet citizen) without reservation; the crimes of the Nazis had been too massive for that. Official documents had to reassure her. Now that Mischka's study in Germany pointed to a convenient use of an existing exchange program, she could understand the choice of her beloved and write about it with "relief."

But is the exchange program as immaculate as Fitzpatrick suggests? After all, it can also be perceived as a product of the Nazis' racial delusions. I don't think Casper would have been so easily persuaded.

When I oppose Fitzpatrick and Casper in this way (in a fictional arena, I admit), then the facts always fall in two directions. Or, to quote E.H. Carr again: "By and large, the historian will get the kind of facts he wants."

Fitzpatrick's bravery is that by committing herself to Misha's history, she dares to challenge the demands of her profession as a historian. In the candid article "Writing History/Writing about Yourself: What's the Difference?" she elaborates on this. Her training as a historian dates back to the 1950s. It was only natural for a historian then to strive for "objectivity" and to write as if it were a "view of nowhere." She also had the temperament for this, she writes with striking honesty: "Feeling detached came naturally to me (and not just as a historian), so I was going to stick with it." The personal could only disrupt her research, so it was important not to be affected by it.

When Fitzpatrick felt the need to write her own history, in autobiographical memoirs about her father (a renowned socialist activist in Australia) and her time working in the Soviet archives, she still intended to treat her personal memories in the same way as she was accustomed to researching historical sources. Her work in the Soviet Union had made her chronically skeptical about archival records. Stalin preferred to orchestrate the archives for future historians, which he called "archival rats." If Fitzpatrick wanted to use her personal memories as a "primary source," she would also have to face them with the same suspicion as she had done with Stalin's archival documents. Every memory had to be checked, even if they were hers and she saw no reason to distrust them.

All the more, she was shocked when she discovered that many of her memories were not shared by others at all or were even directly contradicted: "I was startled by the discrepancies of the various oral accounts and documents, and even more by the fact that things that I subjectively believed — *knew* — to be really important in my life had somehow not made it into the historical record." She realized that she had to radically adjust her attitude towards her own memories as a "primary source" when she learned that a song she had heard a friend sing in her memory in 1958 had only been composed two years later: "So my memory misdated Camilla's song, and on top of that, I passed the false memory on to her, making two mistaken witnesses — but that does not mean the singing of the song and the emotions associated with it did not happen." On the contrary, the recall of an emotion turned out to be more important in writing her personal history than the historically correct dating. The emotion *was* the event.

Even though she meticulously checked her memories, was she still a historian, Fitzpatrick wondered? The interesting thing is that she had the audacity to bend the question to the role of the historian in the process of historiography. Every historian has a "personal subtext," as Fitzpatrick calls it, which inevitably interferes with his or her research. She is not saying it in that many words, but I suspect she realizes that many historians also try to find answers to the issues that consciously or unconsciously shape their own lives. And have their answers determined by their life's view.

When every historiography is a disguised self-investigation of the historian, what do Casper's unveilings about Mekas tell us about himself? What anxieties are hidden in them, what insecurities? What motivates the moral stance of his article? These are issues that are hardly ever raised, and certainly not by the historian himself. They get lost in that voice from nowhere, which has to corroborate the objectivity of his story, even if he writes "I" so often.

In Fitzpatrick's checking of personal memories (those of herself and others), the objective is not to contradict or correct them. She tries to "understand" the people she writes about: "... how their minds work, why they think they do the things that they do, what they see as their options." To which she adds: "That is not what a prosecutor does, or, for that matter, a counsel for the defense."

She doesn't want to denounce nor defend the people whose life she describes. Which doesn't mean she doesn't feel the pressure of a weighty loyalty. Even though she wanted to describe the complexity and uncomfortable contradictions in her social activist father's life, the commitment to reconcile with him should not be called into question. For Misha, this was even more true: "I am not sure that [...] I would have been prepared to go wherever my data took me, if it seemed to diminish Misha. I certainly would not have been prepared to change my opinion of my subject in the process of writing."

You can, of course, attribute that to the special bond Fitzpatrick had with Michael Danos, her Misha. Casper didn't have that kind of tie with Mekas. Still, it's quite possible that he was initially determined to start his research generously. "My interest in Biržai grew out of my interest in Mekas," he wrote in his email. Mekas's personal history suggested to him that he investigate life in a medium-sized city in Lithuania during the Second World War. What could possibly go wrong with that?

At some point in his research, Casper lost his sympathy and patience: "... the republication of *I Had Nowhere to Go*, with its wholly insufficient depiction of the war and his role in wartime publications, necessitated further clarification and discussion. I hoped that Mekas would address the war years more frankly and honestly than he had before but he was not able to do so." One can hear a sincere disappointment in it.

Casper and Mekas, it feels more and more like the story of a failed relationship. Perhaps due to two conflicting personalities: Mekas the egocentric Fluxus genius versus Casper the perfectionist literalist. Perhaps Casper's deepest disappointment was that the man he found in Lithuanian archives was not the man he had admired in New York.

admiration

Fitzpatrick's loyalty to Misha is nourished by love. My loyalty to Mekas comes from admiration and the desire to hold onto the man who gave me some important lessons with his *Movie Journal.* When I re-read those columns while I was writing this, I was amazed at how literally I had been able to reproduce them — they had become part of myself. But there is an important difference between admiration and worship. Admiration is healthy, worship does not tolerate criticism. If you admire, you can also be disappointed. Worship knows no way back; it is total. The disappointed worshiper falls into an existential abyss.

In his life, Mekas is often and intensely admired, but also fervently worshiped. His status as a victim of both Nazism and communism had to do with that. Mekas made little effort to nuance that image. Not only did he allow himself to be charmed by it, but he also seemed to start believing in it himself. It became an important part of his identity. To the irritation of Michael Casper, who admired the artist, but discovered that this admiration could not extend to the man in Lithuania during the Second World War. That is, if that artist wanted to cling to the image of himself as a victim, making an equivalence of some kind to the victimhood of the Jews in Lithuania. I think it is telling that Casper's irritation was to a large extent fueled by a piece of work that was unreservedly driven by worship — a piece of work that precisely traced back to the period he had so meticulously researched.

Scottish visual artist Douglas Gordon was pleased to be friends with Mekas and hang out with him at film festivals. In 2016, he used *I Had Nowhere to Go* for a film with the same title, in which he portrays Mekas's experiences in the Second World War and as a Displaced Person. Generously and benevolently. Which is probably a mild description of how Gordon wanted to relate to his friend and hero.

Gordon has Mekas read excerpts from the diary and complements them with interviews. Surrounding Mekas's characteristic voice (the Lithuanian accent) he constructs a soundscape of rolling tanks, bomb attacks, crossfire, sounds of ships, the rustling of the wind. This "radio show" mostly unfolds under a monochrome black, white or red image. Occasionally, in grubby Van Gogh colors, we see someone cooking or squashing potatoes, a chimpanzee in a zoo, the fresh foliage of a tree, or the out of focus image of Mekas playing his accordion in his loft. Some of these images are probably references to Mekas's quotes: "You can live on a simple potato and survive" is the advice of a family member just before the flight to Germany, and "Ah, you are fools," Mekas scolds visitors of a virtually deserted zoo in post-war Germany as they mock the only surviving chimp.

You can interpret the sound fragments and the images as traces of memory, snippets that emerge from the unknowable black of the past. The script doesn't follow the chronology of the diaries, but arranges them associatively. The film has no intention of being the factual representation of a history, but rather of being the interpretation of it. By disconnecting the anecdotes from their chronology, Gordon tries to lift them to an iconic level. He unreservedly presents Mekas as a survivor of Nazism and communism, and makes no effort to deepen or investigate his story.

The last thing Gordon wants is to pose as a truth-finding historian. He pays homage to a friend, as he is of course entitled to do, but unlike Fitzpatrick he doesn't allow himself any doubt. Under the guise of Art, the uncritical evocation of the diary ends in a shameless hagiography. Gordon's goal is worship; his film is a religious work of art. You don't have to be like Casper to be annoyed by it.

Jonathan Jones, critic of *The Guardian* characterizes the film as "a high-class piece of perverse nostalgia porn"; with which I believe he says not one word of a lie. Jones is reviewing the film two years before the publication of Casper's article, but already seems to sense that Mekas's history and that of Lithuania must be more ambiguous than Gordon's uncritical appropriation would have us believe: "What this film needs are facts. The realities of mass murder and human displacement need to be shown as only cinema can — and that takes work, research, curiosity. If Douglas Gordon wants to make a great film to compare with Claude Lanzmann's *Shoah* he needs to leave his editing suite and go out into landscapes still stained with human ash."

The comparison with *Shoah* comes out of the blue, but may have been rooted in Jones's criticism because of the last excerpt on the soundtrack, which Gordon seems to want to give a programmatic value. In 1953, Mekas describes a nightmarish night, haunted by voices and sounds from the past, in which this phrase appears: "... there is a sounding in his ears, a laugh he just heard, a heavy thumping noise of earth falling on mass graves ...." Neither Gordon nor Jones could have suspected that at that time a young American historian was inquisitive about the facts relating to exactly that sound.

In his version of *I Had Nowhere to Go*, Gordon crushes his friend Mekas under the desire to create Great Religious Art. It is counterproductive. In his article in the *NYRB* and the email he wrote to me, Casper explicitly mentions the film as an instigation to expose his findings. In his eyes, Gordon's "further canonizing" of Mekas's life story had to be stopped. Perhaps Gordon was not the friend Mekas could have wished for after all.

Douglas Gordon lost himself in worship. Admiration should in no way have hindered an affectionate and nuanced image of his hero. This was proven by the American-Dutch couple Sarah Payton and Chris Teerink in 2007 with their film *In the Shadow of the Light*. Payton and Teerink certainly did not lack sympathy or feelings of admiration, but it did not prevent them from looking for the Mekas behind the Fluxus mask. Their film contains moments that draw Mekas's personality for me more sharply than what he has revealed about himself in all his films.

In the Shadow of the Light is both a portrait of Mekas and his life's work Anthology Archives, the largest and most important film archive of experimental American cinema. Mekas proudly shows the shelves with films by Maya Deren, Andy Warhol, Stan Brakhage, Kenneth Anger, Jack Smith, Ken Jacobs — for mainstream film audiences probably no household names, but for fervent cinephiles comparable to what Georgia O'Keeffe, Pablo Picasso, Jackson Pollock, Jean-Michel Basquiat or Tracy Emin mean for the visual arts. Mekas opens boxes of paper archives, from which, like a treasure hunter, he pulls out unique collages by Joseph Cornell. His hand fondly glides past an immense collection of film magazines from all over the world, collected through years of exchange. If his charisma has brought about anything, then this repository of the avant-garde, where anyone with serious intentions is welcome to make use of it.

If I hadn't sent Michael Casper's article to Chris, this book would probably never have been written. I remembered the film he had made with Sarah, and because I felt the need to share my confusion with others, I thought of him. The article didn't leave Chris untouched. He wrote back to me: "When Sarah and I made our film it was difficult after a few weeks, because Mekas was primarily funny. Which is nice, but not for a whole film. Then he gave us his *I Had Nowhere to Go,* which is still in our living room. After we'd read that, we could move on. At some point he writes, when he's in a camp in Germany, that for him the only way to continue on in this world is to play the clown. I had to think of that when I read Casper's article. Jonas who, like any true clown, also carries a great sadness or darkness in him."

In the Shadow of the Light initially shows a Mekas who seems to have built a wall of grumpiness, detachment and evasiveness between himself and the camera of his guests. Which feels strange for the man who himself is filming everything and doesn't seem to exercise any restraint in doing so. Until something cracks.

In his office of Anthology Archives, which is packed with books, magazines, newspapers, letters and unopened parcels, Mekas is visited by an Italian poet. Mekas, of whom we've seen previously that he's constantly being disturbed in the chores he's trying to finish, welcomes the poet kindly but reservedly. Till the timid Italian hands him a picture he took years ago in Mekas's loft. The photo overwhelms Mekas, as he is in the middle of moving to a new apartment in Brooklyn. "Look, a picture of my place the way it was," he says and shows it to the filmmakers' camera. We see a long wall hidden over its full length behind a bulging bookcase. It's the loft I know from *As I Was Moving Ahead Occasionally I Saw Brief Glimpses of Beauty* — the happy family years.

"Now the wall. No more books," Mekas explains. "I moved them to Brooklyn. Three hundred boxes." The sight of the house he has left moves him. And then it happens. Mekas hides his eyes from the gaze of the camera, rubs off his tears, bends his head and starts searching for something in his bag. A sweater comes out, a sachet and then, finally, a small video camera. Mekas starts filming the photo, using the device to shield his emotions.

I think of the nine suitcases with books with which Mekas arrived in New York in 1949. Could they still have been there? I recall the cheerful family images, all those years that Mekas lived here with his wife and children. And I think of the Bolex camera that, I read in his diary, he bought with two hundred borrowed dollars on the 1st of May in 1950 — to keep the world at bay with it?

Until now, Mekas was hiding behind a clownish mask. Chris and Sarah wanted to look for that part of their main protagonist that was hidden behind it. Something that they (and we spectators) hoped would occasionally break through the mask. When Mekas wipes his tears away, a small crack appears in the fleece. To close again at lightning speed, hiding behind his camera.

Another scene reveals the why of Mekas's reticence. Now he is visited by an Italian student who intends to write a thesis on Jack Smith, a cult figure of the American avant-garde, who made the lives of the friends who took care of him, especially Alan Ginsburg, impossible because of his love of alcohol and hallucinogenic drugs. Anthology Archives preserves the film archive of the unruly genius. The student, clearly still searching for a general denominator for the frenzied and uncatalogical film material he has been privileged to watch, drops the word "documentary."

"It's footage," Mekas corrects him as if being bitten, "footage, not documentary."

And there he sees a chance. With a skewed eye to the filmmakers who are making a documentary about him, he explains that the term has a long tradition in film history. It refers to films that are made to reveal everything, but then also "everything" about a subject. To which he adds in one breath: "It's the kind of film I hate."

The message is clear. Don't expect me, filmmakers

from the Netherlands, to disclose myself to you, or that you will manage to "tell all about me," no matter how long you chase me with your camera. What there is to tell about me, you can see. You won't get any further than the outside. Because there's no more than that. If you don't get that, you don't understand my films.

The paradox is, of course, that in our perception of that scene with the photo of his loft, Mekas actually did reveal something. I see the Mekas who has to abandon a home again and doesn't know how to deal with that emotion. Of course, there is more to tell about him, but the fact that he uses the camera as a shield explains something of all those kilometers of filmstrips with which he has documented his life. He keeps the world at a distance, so as not to have to open parts of himself. Which surprises me of an oeuvre that presents itself as so wild and anarchistic and blatant. Has all this self-presentation been nothing more than an ingenious smokescreen, a big vanishing trick?

It is exciting to see that in *In the Shadow of the Light* Mekas tries to avoid the filmmakers and how they eventually manage to enter his mind, materialized in an even more specific space than Anthology Archives.

Sarah and Chris gain access to Mekas's small studio, where he keeps his film material and where he has his editing set. To the filmmakers among the spectators, that editing set is a rare primitive device, which invites you to literally let the film pass through your hands. The image appears on a small screen on the wall, no bigger than that of a laptop. It is a unique device, designed as a prototype in 1965, but no one was interested and Mekas was allowed to keep it. All his films have been edited with it. Two film reels, a box with a faint lamp and a crank to rotate the film by hand. Editing is a tactile activity, finding the right cutting point with your fingers. Mekas likes the device because, as he says, it is "polite" for his reversal film that comes out of his camera as a positive image and therefore is a fragile original, comparable to slides. It is only when Mekas has edited the image strip that he makes a working copy of it and brings together image and sound on a classic Moviola.

The Moviola is stored deep in a remote corner of the long narrow room. Timbered scaffolding along the wall carries sloppily stacked film cans. On the bottom shelf Mekas keeps his four worn Bolexes. One for every decade, he smiles. Whatever they've seen, Mekas's eyes have also seen. Used and used up. The tabletop is covered with screws, little levers, empty film cans and reels, a film splicer.

Mekas records his voice-overs with an antiquarian cassette recorder, a portable consumer model that hasn't been new since the 1970s. Loud, audible clicks when he presses the recording buttons. The small microphone fits three times in the palm of his hand. Old cassettes with almost indecipherable inscriptions surround the device. It looks like a toy, especially for those who have become accustomed to today's sound studios, where the digitized recording techniques clean up every unwanted sound inaudibly. On this device, Mekas's voice cannot but drown in a sea of white noise, even though he waits until night for his recordings when the world around him is silent. A complex cinematic body of work, which challenges our physical and mental perception to the extreme, is pieced together here in the most basic of conditions.

Daylight never enters the studio. A single desk lamp puts Mekas in a heavy chiaroscuro, which contributes to the impression that we are entering the caverns of his mind here. If this is Mekas's mind, then more as a metaphor for an unspeakable secret than for lucid daydreams. The studio feels like a highly personal memory machine, an archive lacking any order, where when the light is dimmed, the shadows of the past flicker on a small screen.

And then there is again such a moment in which my image of Mekas is sharpening. The camera greedily zooms in on a small, oval portrait in black and white hung above the screen. It is Mekas's mother, who has been looking at her son from her silent picture all these years. She has watched over him as he viewed the images he filmed, sorted, selected and edited. There his kids passed by as if he recalled his own childhood: "I guess I was filming my own memories, my own childhood as I was filming your childhood."

Did he seek her approval?

When he visited her in Lithuania after twenty-seven years, she told him that after the war, the secret police of the Soviets had for months been posted every night at their farm to wait for him, sure as they were that he would come back. Then the same might have happened to him as happened to his father a few years later: tortured to death during a police interrogation. She could only hope that he wouldn't return.

Details mark our lives. It's also the details that mark what a film has to tell us. Filming the small, oval portrait of Mekas's mother in his studio tears off the mask one last time and offers us a glimpse of the "real" Mekas, immersed in melancholy, sick with nostalgia — mummy, mummy on the wall...?

When I was writing this, an indeterminate melancholy suddenly overwhelmed me — I was back in the small room in Vicenza at the Madonnas with child and my mother's anxious grip. When did Mekas's memories of happiness and loss become my memories?

settle the scores

Is this, then, the image I would like to end with? The melancholic Mekas, whose nostalgia has planted itself in me? Is that the Jonas Mekas that I have secured for myself?

Many Jonases have already appeared in these pages, and I played them all out as it suited me. First of all the solipsist, which may be a posh word for egocentric or smug. With that, I thought I could express a certain distance: don't think, reader, that my admiration equals uncritical worship. Also a sincere, gentle Mekas passed by, the nostalgia machine with which I identified myself the easiest (a matter of age I assume, the older I get, the more paradisiacal my youth imposes itself upon me). The tormented Mekas of course was there, as was the angry one. That Jonas was nuanced by the helpful one, the wise one, and the funny one. The Fluxus jester was the one who was most fanatically embraced by the international art world, especially when Mekas, with his rising age, gained the appearance of a Zen master. In it I recognize mechanisms that I do not consider to be among the most sympathetic in the art world. The question is whether the Gordons and Obrists were ultimately the "good" friends for Mekas, although that sounds, I realize, rather corny and paternalistic.

And then there was Mekas the liar, the man who had closed certain doors to his memories or against better judgment tried to keep them closed. The stuttering man in the oral history interview for the USHMM didn't help me get rid of that image. That's where I met the tarnished Jonas. If there are people who think that this interview has rehabilitated Mekas and that Casper's article has been sufficiently refuted with it, they've never watched the full six hours. More than ever, I understood that the body also speaks and that this doesn't have to be in sync with the words someone utters.

Following the publication of the article in the *NYRB*, Mekas wrote in a letter to his friends that Casper has "invented" him. How many Jonases did I invent? Which ones I have constructed, whether or not based on directions of Casper or others, of his films and public appearances, his diary and columns, my observations thereof, my interpretations and my imagination? Each one the result of a reduction, ignoring the anomalies that didn't fit — that is, I'm afraid, a guideline that can hardly be avoided by anyone who writes.

I know about the existence of that letter because Jim Hoberman wrote about it on his website. He leaves it open as to whether he received it personally. The letter "circulates" among friends, to whom Hoberman doesn't want to consider himself fully, even though he has known Mekas for a long time, as a colleague at *The Village Voice* and as a neighbor.

On his website, Hoberman explains to an anonymous editor why, after reading Casper's article, he can't review Mekas's new book *Conversations with Film-Makers*. He makes it sound as if Casper has opened his eyes to a secret he may have suspected, but could never fathom. Hoberman comes from a secular

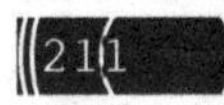

New York Jewish background and wrote an important book on the history of Yiddish film. Maybe that's why he brings up some clumsy statements by Mekas from his own archive, about Hitler's favorite film director Leni Riefenstahl (on which friend Susan Sontag in 1975 already admonished him in "Fascinating Fascism," ironically in *NYRB*'s pages); and about *Jud Süss*, Veit Harlan's anti-Semitic propaganda film in which Mekas said he and his friends, seeing that film during the war, thought they recognized a defense of the Jews. Hoberman's piece balances on the brink of a reckoning, as if he needed a free pass to finally speak about his longstanding discomfort with Mekas's fickle personality.

Did he have any reason to feel uncomfortable about Mekas? That's where it gets tricky, because Mekas published Hoberman's first articles in *The Village Voice*, where he would continue to be a film critic for thirty-five years. Mekas also had him curate programs for Anthology Archives and helped him with the conservation of the films of Jack Smith, the underground filmmaker of, among many others, *Flaming Creatures*. For screening that film in 1964, Mekas was arrested on charges of showing pornography, making the film a flagship of taboo-breaking films of the 1960s.

I recognize the "helpful" Jonas, who all too often made an effort for the "good" causes in the film world: standing up against censorship, offering young talented filmmakers or writers a stage, preserving films that the major archives don't take seriously. It is clear that Hoberman also recognizes this Jonas and feels indebted. Like no other, he knows what Mekas has meant for the American avant-garde cinema, precisely the films Hoberman admires and likes to write about. In that sense, they were allies who stood for the same cause.

The open letter on his website can also be read as a farewell to an important but arduous teacher. Hoberman can't deny Mekas's influence, but everyone knows the moment when you finally have to go your own way, no matter how difficult it is to break free. Maybe it has relieved Hoberman that he doesn't owe Mekas any more thanks, that he didn't have to cover up all those little irritations sticking to that mercurial personality with the cloak of love anymore, like his "eccentric right-wing politics," which must have been hard to bear for the classic liberal that Hoberman is in all his fibers.

Breaking away from a major role model is of course not without its pains. Hoberman learns that Mekas — to put it mildly — is not happy with his public rejection. Which in turn hurts Hoberman (but what else did he expect, I wonder). In his In Memoriam in *The New Yorker* with the significant title "My Debt to Jonas Mekas," he writes: "When I saw Jonas at the Museum of the Moving Image, late last year — we were together on a panel of former *Village Voice* film critics — he didn't look well. I felt terrible. We barely spoke to each other, but I was glad to be able to make a public acknowledgment of my debt to him."

Hoberman, an astute film critic I admire, can't cope with Mekas's unpredictability on which every reduction rebounds. In the open letter, still full of Casper's article, he writes: "He's a sophisticated naive; a self-described dreamer and a hard-headed tactician; an opponent of authority who operated from a succession of power bases; selfless yet self-absorbed; a farm boy adept at hobnobbing with the rich and privileged; a man fervently attached to his roots yet largely self-invented." In *The New Yorker*, immediately after his death, this becomes more by way of a question: "Was he a sly peasant, a sophisticated cosmopolitan, a wise fool, an international man of mystery?"

My bond with Mekas doesn't have the personal dimension it had for Hoberman. My loyalty to him is not affected by career opportunities or his far-reaching readiness to help. In that sense, I owe Mekas nothing. Moreover, not having a Jewish background like Hoberman, I cannot perceive Mekas's forgetfulness as a personal betrayal. Yet I share Hoberman's confusion. I would have liked Mekas to remain the hero he was to me as a young man after I read his *Movie Journal*. I wasn't waiting for the multi-headed monstrosity I can't get a grip on. I wished for a clear and unambiguous character — that he was too human for that, too "real," too ambiguous, I found hard to digest. Why on earth for?

I suspect that the extremes were playing against me. My hero simply was not allowed to be a liar. If I wanted to save the hero, I had to neutralize the liar. Of course, that was not at all a necessity, but then why is it so difficult to accept both sides of his personality? My reduction got in the way. I dreamed of Mekas's life as a clear, unambiguous novella, to discover that it was too real for a novella. It took a shock to recognize and to name Mekas's many sides.

Of course this is not fair to Mekas: to the genuine one, the real one, the one that existed to him, and only himself. Everyone can invent his own Jonas. There are enough leads with which you can make any portrait of him. It is our only way to relate to others. We produce a portrait and only reluctantly adjust it — until new information changes everything.

Had I left it at Casper's article, I would have rejected Mekas in a single breath. I would have let him crash without mercy. Fortunately I didn't do that. By scrutinizing Casper's article to the letter, I got to know another Mekas, erratic and unpredictable, with unsuspected sides, inconsistent and steadfast, amiably generous and annoyingly self-centered. Human and all too human.

Does that release me from a judgment or a conviction of his deeds? I am neither a prosecutor nor a judge. I discovered that in every historian there is something of the two. What presents itself as an account of the facts almost always implies a judgment, if not a conviction, in which the sentence consists of making the incriminating facts known to the world. The person who collects the facts resembles the public prosecutor. The one who arranges the facts into a sound story assumes the role of judge. History combines both positions. It is a form of jurisdiction disguised as science. From that perspective, I tried to be Mekas's lawyer in this essay, although I was not always a reliable one and often lost sight of my client's interests. I got a richly variegated Mekas in return. But did that bring him justice?

My relationship with Casper, the supplier of all that incriminating research and the historical judge on duty, so to speak, has become no less ambiguous in the course of writing this book. I was often reminded of the razor-sharp opening sentences with which Janet Malcolm, in *The Journalist and the Murderer*, describes the relationship between the journalist and his subject: "Every journalist who is not too stupid or too full of himself to notice what is going on knows that what he does is morally indefensible. He is a kind of confidence man, preying on people's vanity, ignorance or loneliness, gaining their trust and betraying them without remorse." In this sense, the role of the historian does not differ much from that of the journalist.

Both are vampires of the past of their subjects, whether recent or long ago. No matter how uncomfortable the facts may be, the journalist and the historian will reveal them without remorse (what Sheila Fitzpatrick calls the historian's Hippocratic Oath).

Gradually I realized that I had nothing to oppose Casper's hard facts. Mekas worked for newspapers which had been brought into line with Nazi occupying forces. In these papers appeared anti-Semitic articles. I didn't have to browse through the newspaper layers myself to believe that. But did he share those anti-Semitic thoughts? Casper has not found any proof of this.

Mekas's silence about the Biržai massacre is more difficult. I can believe that he looked away, like most of his compatriots. I can also believe that he was ashamed of it, and of his countrymen, and therefore remained silent. But is silence always an admission of guilt? Perhaps he was ashamed because he felt powerless.

Mekas made things difficult for himself as a "suspect," because behind his silence (or, more accurately, his silence at most times) seemed to be a stubborn denial. Mekas had not observed the mass murder of 2,400 Jews in Biržai, or at least had no memory of it, he claimed. Casper could not forgive Mekas for the latter. This is not a factual finding, but a moral judgment. As a historian, Casper leaves his role as a prosecutor or a judge, to become a columnist of public opinion. This is not to say that I can't share Casper's annoyance, but I do wonder whether he played the game fairly. His tone is one of suggestive voicing. A moral judgment requires a different assessment than a historical or journalistic disclosure. In my opinion, Casper has too few facts for that.

In the course of my research, I found this increasingly uncomfortable. Casper challenged me not to judge the facts but Mekas's character. Did he give me enough material to carry my verdict? And what about the readers of the *NYRB*? Who, after reading this article, leaf fleetingly through another article, but later, when Mekas's name pops up somewhere, will think: Wasn't that the man who...?

When I was wrapped up in my close reading of Casper's article, I often wondered why the *NYRB* wanted to publish it. In the magazine market, that wasn't self-evident. Hoberman states that two years earlier, a version of the article had been "fact-checked and legally approved" by *The Nation*, but in the end was not published without reason given. When Hoberman asks editor-publisher Katrina vanden Heuvel why the piece has been withdrawn, she claims she has "no clear recollection" of it. "Selective memory is at the heart of the Mekas affair," Hoberman comments dryly. I guess *The Nation* made a simple assessment: are the "facts" worth sacrificing a hero from the artistic left? I suspect that *The Nation* would have been less prudent with Charlton Heston or John Milius.

The article eventually was published in the *NYRB* with Ian Buruma as editor-in-chief. I imagine that the editorial staff discussed it at length, as the *NYRB* also has a readership that is part of Mekas's cultural circles. It wasn't that difficult to get Buruma's email address, because we share the same Dutch publisher. The answer came promptly (in my translation from the Dutch): "My reasons for publishing the article about Mekas are not complex. It was an interesting article that shed new light on the life and work of the filmmaker. He was old and perhaps it was painful for him to read, but I don't believe that that should guide an editor. Something is worthwhile, or not. And I thought the piece was well worth it. I'm sorry I couldn't give you a better or more interesting answer to your question."

I was shocked by the simplicity of the answer. Is it really that uncomplicated to deal with someone's reputation? Could you trade so easily "worthwhile" for "painful to read"? Did Buruma really not feel any qualms about Casper's attack on Mekas's memory?

When I had asked my editor for his email address, she gave me the Dutch translation of *A Tokyo Romance*, Buruma's last published book. I was eager to read it, because ironically, he was one of my other heroes. His first publications on Japan (originally written in Dutch) had been very important to me. These memoirs promised a glimpse of his life in

Tokyo when he wrote them. They had helped to shape my ideas about Japan profoundly, which eventually resulted in the feature film *Felice... Felice...*, entirely spoken in Japanese. I was also pleasantly surprised to read that American author, filmmaker and film historian Donald Richie had played an important role in his life. It brought back a precious memory to me, very vividly, as if a new layer of fondant was added to it.

In 1994, I visited Tokyo to persuade the Japanese film company Shochiku to participate in a film program for the Netherlands Filmmuseum (now Eye) and other European film archives. I also made an appointment with Donald Richie, who at the time was the most important historian of Japanese film and had lived most of his life in Japan. I traveled with Céline, my beloved. Richie welcomed us in an establishment described by Buruma as his favorite meeting place: plenty of sweet cakes, exotic coffee, and cute Japanese schoolgirls giggling at fancy tables. Everything was charm about Donald, and Céline was immediately enchanted. He was extremely pleased when he learned that we were staying in a small guesthouse in Ueno, one of the more traditional neighborhoods of Tokyo. Did we notice the telephone wires there, he asked, which made him think of the rain streaks in Hiroshige's prints? It was enjoyable and polite, especially when we told him that we were intending to follow parts of his travels he wrote about in *The Inland Sea*. After the pastries, he insisted on taking us to the Ueno Park to admire the lotus pond. We looked out over the green foliage, talked about the pink flowers and how they also were reminiscent of Japanese prints.

Buruma's memoirs, however, gave me a new perspective on this memory. It made me understand that the pond meant more to Richie than his nostalgia for Japanese beauty. In the 1970s and '80s, the pathway around it was a notorious place for quick, anonymous homosexual contacts. Buruma recounts that Richie liked to go there. Japan offered him the possibility to indulge his bisexuality in an inconspicuous way. Our outing with this terse gentleman (seventy at the time, who seemed more English than American) suddenly spun a quarter of a turn in my memory: Richie had brought us to his favorite cruising spot. Was it a hint to us, or did he just go there, after we had parted at nightfall, for other things than films and woodblock prints? Or was it simply nostalgia, and did the two Dutch give him an excuse to go back to that place of long gone cravings?

Frankly, I conjecture about most of the facts of that meeting, but the feeling came back with the greatest ease from how Buruma described Richie. I wonder from whom my memory of Richie and the visit to Ueno Park really stems: how much Buruma has blended in with my own recollections?

Buruma can't be surprised, because in his Acknowledgments in *A Tokyo Romance* he writes:

"Naturally, memories are fragmentary, fallible, and subject to constant change, as the story of one's own life (never coherent in the first place) keeps being reedited in the mind." He can't fall back on diaries, letters or too many pictures of himself, he explains: "All I can claim is I have written this account of my Tokyo years as best as I can remember them. I have not consciously made things up. But it is, for all the reasons mentioned above, as well as for literary reasons, an edited version."

Does Buruma allow himself that degree of freedom (which seems only self-evident to me), which in the "interesting article" Casper denies Mekas? Would this "disclaimer" still apply when someone checks Buruma's memories and comes up with new "facts"? Has he then simply "edited" his memories? Or will he kindly "revise" them, even if it's "unpleasant" to read?

Maybe Buruma was not in the best mood for my email. Shortly before, he had left the *NYRB* with slamming doors, after his editorial staff had distanced themselves from him. He had published an article by the Canadian musician and radio host Jian Ghomeshi, who was accused of sexual harassment and assault and was provided space in the magazine to tell what his life had looked like after those accusations. Buruma posted the article without editorial clarification or contextualization (as with all articles in the magazine), which turned out to be an underestimation of the outrage #MeToo had caused in the cultural world. Allowing an "offender" to speak uncommented expressed a liberality that Buruma's editorial staff could not forgive him.

I recall this because I sense in Casper's article a similar moral imperative that characterizes the #MeToo era, of which comedienne Sarah Silverman provocatively referred to as "righteousness porn." I think it is not without irony that Casper's article about Mekas's "war past" echoes the same desire to "render justice" and thus publicly position oneself on the good side of the moral line. If Casper lacks something, then empathy for the young Mekas in a time and circumstances of moral confusion. I often wondered if he didn't use today's moral standard a bit too easily and showed little feel for what it was like to live in Lithuania between 1939 and 1945. "History cannot be written unless the historian can achieve some kind of contact with the mind of those about whom he is writing," writes E.H. Carr in his philosophy of historiography. I would have liked to ask Casper more about that. And hear more about that from Buruma.

Yet, at the same time, it was not so difficult to maneuver myself into a position of moral indignation and express my own righteousness, which can be read back often enough in the previous pages. To imagine what happened in the forest of Astravas, I read *Ordinary Men* by Christopher Browning, which describes meticulously how similar murders as in

Lithuania were carried out in Poland. Over the following days, I wandered around nauseously. Realizing that each of the 2,400 victims had been killed with a shot to the neck, 2,400 dry clicks in one day, the blood-soaked mud, babies screeching, the robbing of valuables, the shoes of the dead, their coats, the stench and the moaning of the half-dead, buried alive — I am not exaggerating, Lithuania was a bloodstained land for the six months of the massacres. Casper knows these stories, and I'm sure he's read a lot more of them than I have. He knew the names of some in the columns of death. He read their newspapers and magazines in the archives, looked at the photographs in them, read their books and noted their optimism about a Jewish home in an independent Lithuania. How difficult it is then to accept that it is possible to live alongside that.

Every human being is the plaything of what can be described afterwards as "the course of events," and during these events (when life is lived), this will mainly be experienced as confusing, uncontrollable and chaotic. Even though each of us is a subsidiary of the great story of history, we simultaneously act independently of it, driven by banal and daily choices, moments of chagrin, hunger, infatuation, euphoria, chance, self-conceit, disinterest.

Disinterest is probably the hardest scourge for those who do historical research: to have to accept that people have actually lived alongside the events — or have tried to do so for as long as possible. Why do I first read the sports section in a newspaper or magazine and only later, if I don't forget, the political analyses, the reports about refugees, forgotten wars, the food bank in the part of town where I don't live? How much different is that from Mekas's poems, which were surrounded by articles that didn't interest him? But is that sufficient to publicly pillory someone?

You could say that Mekas has maneuvered himself into the danger zone by making so blatantly and lavishly his own biography the subject of his art. In this sense, Casper's article is the punishment for his vanity and narcissism. It is also the punishment for his long conduct in life, as his little life's story, told in experimental, headstrong films, became more and more the grand narrative of one of the last remaining survivors of communism and Nazism in the 1940s, culminating in the art film that art star Douglas Gordon made of his diaries. Mekas refrained from nuancing that role himself, thus completing the circle towards narcissism and self-absorption.

Casper refused to let Mekas get away with a faltering memory, or with his egotism. Whoever, like Mekas, has the status of an important witness, has to behave accordingly, Casper states, and, if necessary, must refresh his own memory with historical research, literature, conversations with archival researchers, and if need be, look for his own Fitzpatrick – or Casper. According to Casper, Mekas has made it too easy for himself, hiding behind his highly personal memory, and has complacently leaned into the role that has been attributed to him, without considering whether he could fulfill that role or even deserved it. Modesty would have been to Mekas's credit, is Casper's perpetual suggestion to him.

This means that it is not Mekas's actions that are on trial, but his personality. Or rather, a part of it, because those who come to Mekas's aid mainly refer to his great deeds as an animator of American film culture and being its keeper in Anthology Archives. This is his life in New York, as a patron of the cinephile brotherhood, suggesting that whatever Mekas has done before, he has now paid off with this part of his life. That will certainly have influenced my own leniency towards Mekas as well.

Casper's critics have therefore accused him of "character assassination," which is true in itself. Casper must have known that with his article he inflicted a dagger in Mekas's reputation — in who Mekas was to himself and others. He felt he detected a false image that needed to be adjusted. Not the image of the course of events, but the image Mekas had given himself in it. Mekas was not the person he made everyone believe he had been. I constantly ask myself whether you have to call that a crime or an unforgivable flaw in character, or if it's just something about which you can shrug your shoulders.

I think it's not a crime. Why would you bother someone who is ninety-five with that? Someone who believed he'd finished the novel of his life. Mekas died six months after the article was published. Friends attributed the rapid deterioration in his condition to Casper's article. Which, of course, was meant as a dagger-thrust for Casper. That doesn't alter the anger that could have raged in Mekas during those last six months, as he stubbornly refused to adjust his memories.

I find Mekas's faith in his memory recognizable. The older the recollection and the more often it is retold, the stronger our memory will trust it. Of course there are clusterings in it, mangled events that are wrapped together like a knot of Velcro. Over the years they have become reassuringly lucid and irrefutably true. They are "facts" that you don't give up just like that, even not when someone unexpectedly shows up to unravel the jumble, poke his fingers between the strands, and puts them in a new order that looks much less reassuring than before. Memory will stubbornly cling to the old order, trying to preserve the wholeness of our existence, no matter how unreliable it may seem facing the facts of books and documents and dates. Or, as the historian David Lowenthal impeccably formulates it in an article tellingly entitled "Forging the Past": "As we grow older, we are continually threatened by the truth about ourselves, as about the world; maturation makes liars of us all."

Mekas would not have been ashamed of "the liar in all of us." As an artist he knew the ways of the fictionalization of our lives, it was his daily work. As a filmmaker and novelist, I too know how it works, how events and intentions can be traded to tell a better story. The events or intentions exchanged for the "better ones" disappear into a bottomless reservoir where they lead an invisible existence. Call it our unconscious, or latent memory, or the undercurrents that steer our actions unnoticed. Artists believe in the steering power of that reservoir, even if there is little factual material to be discovered in it. The work of Mekas, his poems and his films, draw incessantly from that reservoir. His films can even be viewed as an attempt to give that reservoir a visible existence; the disorder of his series of images is the expression of it.

Casper is not insensitive to Mekas's artistry. He reads his films, poems and diaries like a trained critic. Yet he does not judge (and convict) the work, but the artist. Casper is the historian and Mekas the artist – both claim their role and believe unconditionally in its absolute priority. That seems to me to be the misunderstanding between the two: the historian and the artist who do not speak the same language.

I can't deny that both protagonists irritated and frustrated me more often than I wanted – they resisted becoming lucid characters in my story. I wanted to comprehend both, which may have made me too indulgent in the eyes of some. I sought the nuance, to discover that it is not in the proverbial middle, but rather resembles a pendulum that refuses to stay on one side of the line. Why is it so difficult to do justice to two seemingly incompatible points of view and simply accept this as a fact of life?

What was it that urged me to continue, anyway? I believe it was Casper's claim that Mekas *was given the authority of a witness, but failed to assume the responsibility that comes with it.* Not the question "what happened?" propelled my investigation, but "how has Mekas been presenting the events — to us, his audience, and to himself?" That turned out to be a broader question than one that only concerned the "little" life story of Jonas Mekas. It was a question about taking responsibility, the pain that honesty demands and the courage to overcome shame, to dare to look yourself in the eye.

I am convinced that the memory of the forest of Astravas has been unbearable for Mekas — that conclusion did not come as a surprise to me. What has come to my mind much sharper (and in that sense came as a surprise) is that the image of the massacre must also have been unbearable for Casper — it tasked him with the mission to save that event from oblivion, even if it meant he had to demolish Mekas's reputation for it. This is the tragedy, in the classical sense of the word, of their dispute. Fate had something else in mind with both protagonists. When their paths crossed, it was impossible not to hurt each other.

* * *

Literature

Adkins, Laura E. "At Shul, We Drink Single Malt: On 'A Fortress in Brooklyn.'" *Los Angeles Review of Books*. May 26, 2021.

Atamukas, Solomonas. "The Hard Long Road to Truth." *Lituanus* 47, no. 4 (Winter 2001).

Beunders, Henri. "Beter achter de rug. Een pleidooi voor vergetelheid." *De Groene Amsterdammer*. October 3, 2018.

Broden, Thomas F. "Toward a Biography of Algirdas Julius Greimas (1917–1992)." *Lituanus* 57, no. 4 (Winter 2011).

Browning, Christopher. "The Personal Contexts of a Holocaust Historian: War, Politics, Trials, and Professional Rivalry." In *Holocaust Scholarship: Personal Trajectories and Professional Interpretations*, edited by Christopher R. Browning, Susannah Heschel, Michael R. Marrus, Milton Shain. London: Palgrave Macmillan, 2015.

———. *Ordinary Men: Reserve Police Battalion 11 and the Final Solution in Poland*. New York: Harper Collins, 1992.

———. *Remembering Survival Inside a Nazi Slave-labor Camp*. New York: W.W. Norton & Co., 2011.

Bult, Jeroen. "Ook Litouwen deed niet mee aan de holocaust." *De Groene Amsterdammer*. January 15, 2020.

Buruma, Ian. *A Tokyo Romance. A Memoir*. London: Penguin, 2018.

Carr, E.H. *What is History?* Harmondsworth: Penguin, 1987.

Casper, Michael. "I Was There." *The New York Review of Books*. June 7, 2018.

———. "On Jonas Mekas: An Exchange." *The New York Review of Books*. July 19, 2018.

———. *Strangers and Sojourners: The Politics of Jewish Belonging in Lithuania, 1914–1940* (PhD thesis, UCLA, 2019). https://escholarship.org/uc/item/6336g000

Casper, Michael and Deutsch, Nathaniel. *A Fortress in Brooklyn: Race, Real Estate, and the Making of Hasidic Williamsburg*. New Haven: Yale University Press, 2021.

Draaisma, Douwe. *Forgetting: Myths, Perils and Compensations*. London: Yale University Press, 2015.

Fitzpatrick, Sheila. "Writing History/Writing about Yourself: What's the Difference?" In *Clio's Lives: Biographies and Autobiographies of Historians*, edited by Doug Munro, John G. Reid. Acton: Australia National University Press, 2017.

———. *Mischka's War: A Story of Survival from War-Torn Europe to New York*. London: I.B. Taurus & Co., 2017.

Gerdžiūnas, Benas. "Is Dutch Holocaust apology relevant to Lithuania?", *Lithuanian Radio and Television* (LRT) website, January 29, 2020.

Gitelman, Zvi (editor). *Bitter Legacy: Confronting the Holocaust in the USSR*. Bloomington: Indiana University Press, 1997.

Hanau, Shira. "In Brooklyn's hipster Williamsburg neighborhood, Hasidic Jews are the real counterculture." *Forward*, June 9, 2021.

Hoberman, Jim. "My Debt to Jonas Mekas." *New Yorker*, January 24, 2019.

———. "Why I cannot review Jonas Mekas's Conversations with Film-Makers." June 30, 2018. http://j-hoberman.com/2018/06/why-i-cannot-review-jonas-mekass-conversations-with-film-makers/

Jones, Jonathan. "*I Had Nowhere to Go* review — Douglas Gordon's fatuous bio-doc of Jonas Mekas." *The Guardian*, September 26, 2016.

Kulikauskas, Andrius. "The World Celebrates Professor Greimas With No Regard for His Victims"; website *Defending History*, November 3, 2017. http://defendinghistory.com/the-world-celebrates-professor-greimas-with-no-regard-for-his-victims/91017

———. "Request for a Moment of Silence." http://www.ms.lt/derlius/requestforamomentofsilence.pdf

Levi, Primo. *If This Is a Man*, translated by Stuart Woolf. Royal Tunbridge Wells: Abacus, 2003.

———. *Shema: Collected Poems of Primo Levi*, translated by Ruth Feldman and Brian Swann. London: Menard Press, 1976.

Lowenthal, David. "Forging the Past." In *Fake? The Art of Deception*, edited by Mark Jones. London: British Museum Publications Ltd., 1990.

MacQueen, Michael. "Lithuanian Collaboration in the 'Final Solution': Motivations and Case Studies." In *Lithuania and the Jews. The Holocaust Chapter, Symposium Presentations.* Washington: USHMM, 2005.

Malcolm, Janet. *The Journalist and the Murderer*. New York: Alfred A. Knopf Inc., 1990.

Matthäus, Jürgen. "Key Aspects of German Anti-Jewish Policy." In *Lithuania and the Jews. The Holocaust Chapter, Symposium Presentations*. Washington: USHMM, 2005.

Mekas, Jonas. "An Address by Jonas Mekas Delivered at Commencement Exercises Philadelphia College of Art June, 11, 1966." https://archive.org/details/commencementaddroomeka

———. *Artist's Book*. Paris: Onestar Press, 2003.

———. *I Had Nowhere to Go*. New York: Black Thistle Press, 1991; Leipzig: Spector Books, 2017.

———. *Movie Journal*. New York: Collier Books, 1972.

———. *My Night Life*. Vilnius: Baltos Lankos P., 2007.

———. *There is No Ithaca: Idylls of Semeniškiai & Reminiscences*; translated by Vyt Bakaitys; Foreword Czeslaw Milosz. New York: Black Thistle Press, 1996.

O'Donoghue, Darragh. "Trembling with Memory: The True Diaries of Jonas Mekas" (Web Exclusive). *Cineaste* XLII, no. 1.

Rieff, David. *In Praise of Forgetting. Historical Memory and Its Ironies*. New Haven: Yale University Press, 2016.

Rosin, Yosef. "Birzh (Biržai), Lithuania." https://kehilalinks.jewishgen.org/birzai/Birzh_1.html

Schwabsky, Barry. "On Jonas Mekas: An Exchange." *The New York Review of Books*, July 19, 2018.

Snyder, Timothy. *Bloodlands: Europe between Hitler and Stalin*. London: Vintage Books, 2011.

———. "Hitler's Logical Holocaust." *The New York Review of Books*, December 20, 2012.

———. "Neglecting the Lithuanian Holocaust." *NYRB* website July 25, 2011. https://www.nybooks.com/daily/2011/07/25/neglecting-lithuanian-holocaust/

Sužiedėlis, Saulius. "The Burden of 1941." *Lituanus, Lithuanian Quarterly Journal of Arts and Sciences* 47, no. 4, Winter 2001.

———. *Historical Dictionary of Lithuania, Second Edition.* Lanham: The Scarecrow Press, Inc., 2011.

Sverdiolas, Arūnas. "Algirdas J. Greimas's Egology." *Actes Semiotiques*, no. 122, 2019.

Todorov, Tzvetan. *Memory as Remedy for Evil* (translation of *Les Abus de la mémoire*). London : Seagull Books, 2010.

Vaartjes, Gé. *Beeld van De Man. Herman de Man (1898–1946), een leven in foto's*. Noorden: Post, 2006.

——. *Herman de Man. Een biografie*. Soesterberg: Aspekt, 1999.

Wagenaar, Willem. *The Popular Policeman and Other Cases: Psychological Perspectives on Legal Evidence*. Amsterdam: Amsterdam University Press, 2005.

Wagner, Kim. "Amritsar, 1919, Letter to the editor." *The London Review of Books*, April 18, 2019.

Internet Sources

Mekas

Jonas Mekas, official website. http://jonasmekas.com

The Angry Dog, Mekas interviewed by Hans-Ulrich Obrist. https://www.serpentinegalleries.org/exhibitions-events/jonas-mekas-conversations-filmmakers

USHMM

"Oral history interview with Jonas Mekas," interview by Ina Navazelskis: June 29 and July 1, 2018, United States Holocaust Memorial Museum oral history collection. https://collections.ushmm.org/search/catalog/irn619022

"Oral history interview with Algimantas Gureckas," interview by Ina Navazelskis: October 14, 2010, United States Holocaust Memorial Museum oral history collection. https://collections.ushmm.org/search/catalog/irn42272

Lithuania

The International Commission for the Evaluation of the Crimes of the Nazi and Soviet Occupation

Regimes in Lithuania. https://www.komisija.lt/en/

Holocaust Atlas of Lithuania. http://www.holocaustatlas.lt/EN/

"The Holocaust in Lithuania – Dr. Christoph Dieckmann": YouTube video with an excellent explanation and analysis of the history of Lithuania during German occupation; the new paradigm in only sixteen minutes. https://www.youtube.com/watch?v=HH2ocwBuFEA

"A new monument was unveiled in Biržai on the site of the massacre of Jews and trees for the rescuers of Jews were planted." https://www.komisija.lt/en/a-new-monument-was-unveiled-in-birzai-on-the-site-of-the-massacre-of-jews-and-trees-for-the-rescuers-of-jews-were-planted/

"Geschichte der Birzaier Juden bis 1945." https://www.birzai.de/ziele/juden/geschichte-der-birzaier-juden.html

Filmography

Walden (Diaries, Notes, and Sketches) (1969), Jonas Mekas

Reminiscences of a Journey to Lithuania (1972), Jonas Mekas

Lost, Lost, Lost (Diaries, Notes and Sketches) (1976), Jonas Mekas

Scenes from the Life of Andy Warhol (1990), Jonas Mekas

As I Was Moving Ahead Occasionally I Saw Brief Glimpses of Beauty (2001), Jonas Mekas

365 Day Project (2007), Jonas Mekas

Correspondences: José Luis Guerin and Jonas Mekas (2011), José Luis Guerin, Jonas Mekas

Outtakes From the Life of a Happy Man (2012), Jonas Mekas

In the Shadow of the Light (2007), Sara Payton, Chris Teerink

I Had Nowhere to Go (2016), Douglas Gordon

George — The Story of George Maciunas and Fluxus (2018), Jeffrey Perkins

acknowledgments

For a variety of reasons, I owe a debt of gratitude to: Anna Abrahams, Aryan Kaganof, Carrie Paterson, Caspar Dullaart, Chris Teerink, Dara Waldron, Esther Polak, Hansje Quartel, Hayo Deinum, Ian Buruma, Ina Navazelskis, Ingrid Harms, John IJkelenstam, Joke Meerman, Jurriën Rood, Marente Bloemheuvel, Marijke Foudraine-Kranenburg, Menno Otten, Michael Casper, Ninon Liotet, Rolf Orthel, Sarah Payton, Tilly Hermans, and most notably Céline Linssen.

Three chapters from this book were adapted into an experimental visual presentation in the digital journal *Herri*.

They are available at:
https://herri.org.za/5/the-forgotten-evil/

about the author

Peter Delpeut (b.1956) is a Dutch author and film-maker. He has written four novels, several essay books on art and film, and two lyrical books about long distance cycling. The Dutch version of *The Big Bend* about his cycling trip from Orlando to Las Vegas enjoyed numerous reprints. For his debut novel in 2007 he was nominated for the Gerard Walschap Prize and awarded the Halewijn Prize. He makes films in many genres: found footage, documentary and features. Many of them are critically acclaimed and prizewinning films. He studied philosophy and film theory, graduating from the Dutch Film Academy in 1984. He served as editor for film magazines *Skrien* and *Versus*. From 1988 to 1995 he worked as curator and deputy-director for the Netherlands Filmmuseum (now Eye), famous at the time for its revolutionary color preservations of films from the silent era. In 2005 a retrospective of his film work was presented in Washington D.C., New York and Berkeley, California. He currently lives in Amsterdam.

www.ingramcontent.com/pod-product-compliance
Lightning Source LLC
Chambersburg PA
CBHW011933050726
47590CB00011B/3270
* 9 7 8 1 9 5 4 6 0 0 0 3 4 *